Business Fundamentals
from
Harvard Business School Publishing

READING FINANCIAL REPORTS, SECOND EDITION

Harvard Business School Publishing

CONTENTS

INTRODUCTION

Welcome to the Business Fundamentals series from Harvard Business School Publishing!

The readings in this collection were developed for the MBA and executive programs of Harvard Business School. These programs rely heavily on the case method of instruction, in which students analyze and discuss firsthand accounts of actual management situations. Students also learn the fundamentals of what managers do: how they measure performance, make choices, and organize their activities. At Harvard Business School, the fundamentals are often taught through background notes, which describe business processes, management techniques, and industries.

The collections in this series are not meant to be comprehensive, but to present the fundamentals of business. Each collection contains several notes, and perhaps an article or two, that provide a framework for understanding a particular business topic or function.

Business is not an exact science. Your own business knowledge comes from your own experiences and observations, accumulated over many years of practice. These collections aim to give you a framework for past and future experiences, using many of the same materials taught at Harvard Business School.

The Business Fundamentals collections are designed for both individual study and facilitated training. If you want to use this collection for self-study, we've provided a summary, outline, learning objectives, and questions for each reading to help you get started. If these readings are part of a training program in your company, you will find them to be a rich resource for discussion and group work.

You can search for related materials on our Web site: www.hbsp.harvard.edu. We hope that your learning experience will be a rich one.

THE ACCOUNTING FRAMEWORK, FINANCIAL STATEMENTS, AND SOME ACCOUNTING CONCEPTS

(W.J. Bruns, Jr. / #9-193-028 / 12 p)

Summary

This note introduces managers to the accounting framework, describes the basic financial statements and how they classify financial information, and briefly explains eleven accounting concepts.

Outline

The Basic Accounting Framework

Assets
Equities ~ Liabilities ?
Assets = Equities
Classifications of Assets and Equities

Basic Financial Statements

The Balance Sheet
The Statement of Income
The Statement of Cash Flows

Accounting Concepts

Learning Objectives

After reading the note and completing the following exercises, managers should be able to:

- Understand what kind of information each basic financial statement (balance sheet, income statement, and cash flow statement) is meant to provide.
- Become familiar with the format and vocabulary of their company's financial statements.
- Recognize how several basic accounting concepts are reflected in financial statements.

1

Questions and Ideas to Consider

Distribute copies of your firm's most recent annual report. (If an annual report is not available, try to obtain copies of the company's latest financial statements, or use the statements provided in the exhibits.)

1. As you read the section on "The Balance Sheet" (pp. 5-7), match each definition with the corresponding item on your firm's balance sheet.

   a) According to the balance sheet, what are your company's largest assets or group of assets? Which assets changed the most from the previous year? Do you know why? What significance might this change have for your department?

   b) What are your company's largest liabilities? Which liabilities changed the most from the previous year? Do you know why? What impact might this change have on your department?

2. As you read the section on "The Statement of Income" (p. 7), match each definition with the corresponding item on your company's income statement.

   a) Is cost of goods sold explained in a footnote? If not, briefly list what contributes to your company's cost of goods sold.

   b) How does your company present operating expenses? What are the major components of its operating expenses?

   c) Has cost of goods sold or SG&A increased as a percentage of revenue compared to last year? Why or why not?

3. As you read the section on "The Statement of Cash Flows" (pp. 7-8), match each definition with the corresponding item on your firm's statement of cash flows.

   a) What are the biggest sources of cash?

   b) What are the biggest uses of cash?

   c) What accounts for the greatest change in cash (i.e., operations, investing activities, or financing activities)?

The Accounting Framework, Financial Statements, and Some Accounting Concepts

Providing information for decisions about the deployment and use of resources in an organization and in the economy is one of the top objectives of accounting and accountants. Over many years, certain formats and procedures for presenting accounting information have come into wide use. Financial statements are based on a framework appropriately called *The Accounting Framework*.

The Basic Accounting Framework

The accounting framework rests on two premises. The first is the idea that it is possible to distinguish an *accounting entity*—the person or organization for which a set of accounts is kept—from other persons or organizations that are associated with it. The second premise is that for any accounting entity, the resources available will be exactly equal to the resources provided by creditors and owners. This second assumption is usually called *the accounting equation* and is written

$$Assets\ =\ Equities$$

The accounting processes of observing, measuring, and reporting are always carried out with an eye to maintaining this fundamental equality of assets and equities.

Assets

In general, assets may be thought of as all things of value that the organization has a right to use. They consist of financial resources, equipment and other physical resources, and other resources having value to the entity. Most business organizations have a wide variety of assets, which they may classify according to common characteristics. Some prevalent financial assets include cash and cash balances in banks, amounts owed to the organization by customers, and marketable securities held by the firm. Operating assets often include land, buildings, equipment used in carrying out the activities of the organization, and inventories of unsold products. Other assets might include such intellectual property as copyrights or patents, conveying exclusive rights to profit from the use of property or process.

Professor William J. Bruns prepared this note as the basis for class discussion.

Equities

The equities in an organization represent claims on its resources or assets. In a crude way, the equities reveal the suppliers of an organization's resources. Some parties provide resources and expect to be repaid; these are creditors. Others contribute resources and thereby become participants; these are owners. Equities of nonowners would include amounts owed to employees or suppliers, amounts owed on short-term loans, and loans represented by other debts of one kind or another. Owners share in both the risks and whatever profits accrue. The equities of owners include the amount of resources that they contributed originally as well as some portion of the earnings that have not been withdrawn by them.

Assets = Equities

The accounting equation demands that in accounting for an organization, the equality of assets and equities must be preserved. Thought of in another way, if the resources owned by an entity increase, the new resources had to have come from somewhere, and that source has a claim against them. If the things of value owned by an organization increase, the corresponding increase either in the amount of obligations or in the equities of owners must be recognized. Likewise, if the things of value owned by an entity decrease, obligations to nonowners may have been satisfied, or the equity of owners may have been reduced.

Classifications of Assets and Equities

Although there are decision situations in which information about total assets or total equities can be useful, in most cases, more detail is desired. Both assets and equities come in very different forms with very different characteristics, as we have already noted. For this reason, it is customary in accounting to adopt a scheme for classifying assets and equities of various types. The classifications can be as large or as small as necessary to achieve the objectives for measuring and reporting. As the number of classifications increases, the cost of measuring, record keeping, and reporting increases, so there is usually an economic constraint that limits the number of classifications actually employed.

The basic accounting equation is commonly expanded to highlight the two major equity classifications:

$$Assets\ =\ Liabilities + Owners'\ Equity$$

Assets — Liabilities = Equity / retained earnings?

This expansion recognizes that there is a fundamental difference between the obligations the organization has to outsiders, or those who are not members or owners, and the obligation it has to owners, or shareholders—those who have invested capital in the organization. In the event the organization is dissolved, obligations to creditors must be met before assets are distributed to owners. This legal distinction provides the basis for this additional classification.

One reason why this expanded form of the accounting equation is used relates to the fundamental distinction between an organization or entity and its owners. The owners contribute capital, but they are not the entity. If the excess of assets over liabilities increases, owners' equity is increased. As long as owners do not make additional capital contributions or withdrawals from the assets of the firm, increases in owners' equity are usually associated with income-generating activities of an organization, whereas decreases usually result from losses.

Basic Financial Statements

The nature and format of financial statements are derived directly from the basic accounting framework and the accounting equation. A *Balance Sheet* (or *Statement of Financial Position*) lists the assets, liabilities, and owners' equity at a specified point in time. An asset-flow statement (the *statement of cash flows* is the most common) summarizes the reasons why a class of assets has increased or decreased over a period of time. A *Statement of Income* (or *Earnings*) explains why the retained earnings classification within owners' equity has changed over a period of time, assuming owners have not taken assets from the firm in the form of dividends.

Although financial statements are prepared in many different formats and may use account classifications that differ substantially, a reader of financial reports who understands the basic accounting equation can usually figure out how to read the financial reports of an organization regardless of the particular reporting scheme that the organization has chosen. The consolidated financial statements of the Coca-Cola Company and Subsidiaries for 1996 provide an illustration of the relationship between the accounting equation and a set of financial reports for a corporation. The Consolidated Balance Sheet (see **Exhibit 1**) illustrates the basic equality between assets and equities. The Consolidated Statement of Income (see **Exhibit 2**) measures how retained earnings were affected by operations before the payment of cash dividends, and the Consolidated Statement of Cash Flows (see **Exhibit 3**) shows why the amount of cash and cash equivalents changed because of operating, investing, and financing activities.

These financial reports provide an outline for reviewing some of the elements that will be found in every set of financial reports of a corporation.

The Balance Sheet

The *Balance Sheet* (or *Statement of Financial Position)* presents a company's financial position as of a specific date, based on measurements made in accordance with *Generally Accepted Accounting Principles* (*GAAP*) or some other reporting basis. By definition, the measured amount of total assets is always equal to the measured amount of liabilities and owners' equity. Except for monetary amounts such as cash, accounts receivable, and accounts payable, the measurements of each classification will rarely be equal to the actual current value or cash value shown. This is due to the fact that most measurements in accounting are made at the time of a transaction that took place in the past, and these historical measurements are retained in the accounts, even though the values of assets and some obligations may increase or decrease with the occurrence of events or passage of time. It is essential to remember that no statement of financial position will ever present the true financial value of an organization or the financial significance of the classifications used in the reports.

The classifications used by the Coca-Cola Company in its Consolidated Balance Sheet (**Exhibit 1**) are typical of those that will be found in the balance sheets of other companies. *Current Assets* include cash and other assets used in operations during the normal operating cycle of the business, or within one year if the operating cycle is shorter than one year. The *normal operating cycle* of a company is that period of time required to acquire services and materials to create a product or service, which is sold to a customer, who then pays for the product or service, thus supplying the cash to begin the cycle again. *Cash and cash equivalents* are measured at their face amounts, whether they are in the possession of the company or deposited in banks. *Marketable securities* represent temporary investments, which can be easily converted to cash if more cash is needed. *Trade accounts receivable* are amounts that are due from customers who have purchased goods or services on credit. *Inventories* typically include materials that will be converted into product, work-in-process inventory, and finished goods that are ready for sale or have not yet been delivered to customers. *Prepaid expenses* include expenditures that have been made to acquire future benefits or services (an insurance policy would be an example), but for which the benefits have not been obtained at the date of the financial reports.

Following the current assets are a number of other assets that are *not* current: that is, they are not expected to be used up within a year, or within the normal operating cycle of the business.

Property, Plant and Equipment represents the cost of long-lived, tangible assets that are used in the company's operations. Land is almost always included at its original cost, while other assets are stated at their original cost less the proportion of original cost that has been included in the expenses of prior periods' operations as depreciation.

Many companies, particularly large companies, have assets that are not used directly in their operations or that they do not have majority ownership of. These are considered "nonoperating" assets and are usually called *Investments*. Coca-Cola has a number of such "investments." *Marketable securities* are securities of other companies similar to the marketable securities in the "Current Assets" section except that *these* securities are expected to be held for a long-term period. *Equity method investments* are also investments in the securities of other companies, but these have to be accounted for somewhat differently (under the *equity method*) because the investor (here, Coca-Cola) owns enough of the companies to have "significant influence" over them (usually presumed to be 20% or more of their outstanding stock but less than 50%). The equity method of accounting essentially records the investor's pro-rata share of all of the earnings of the investee and represents a more elaborate way of accounting for the investment than occurs with ordinary "marketable securities." Other kinds of "investments" (not represented here) might be the cash surrender value of life insurance or special-purpose funds that accumulate cash in a systematic way to meet some specific future needs.

If a company has purchased another company for a price in excess of the fair market value of its identifiable assets, *goodwill* (which represents intangible things like the acquired company's excellent reputation or highly marketable brand names) is assumed to have been acquired and will be recorded as an additional asset.

On the other side of the accounting equation are liabilities and the owners' equity. *Liabilities* are obligations that an organization must satisfy by transferring assets to or performing services for a person or organization at some time in the future. *Current liabilities* are those that an organization expects to satisfy either with assets that have been classified as current or in the course of normal operations or during the following year. Liabilities not falling within these categories are usually shown as *long-term debts* or *other liabilities*.

Shareowners' Equity (or *Stockholders' Equity*) represents the interest of the owners in the organization. Mathematically, its total is always equal to the amount that remains after deducting the total liabilities of the organization from its total assets. Only by coincidence would this amount be equal to the true value of the organization to its owners. Instead, the total is very much an artifact of the measurements and accounting procedures that have been used to record and account for assets and liabilities.

The amount of assets that owners originally committed to the organization (usually cash paid for stock) is usually shown separately in the owners' equity section of the Balance Sheet. In the case of the Coca-Cola Company, that amount consists of *Common stock* with a certain "par value" (which is a nominal, base value) plus *Capital surplus* (often called *Additional paid-in capital*), which represents the money that owners paid for stock in excess of the par value. Once these original assets are turned over to an organization, no further measurements are made, and the market value of the shares representing ownership may differ substantially from the original amount paid by the original owners.

Reinvested earnings (often referred to as *Retained earnings*) shows the accumulated net income of an organization from its origin to the present, after deducting dividends to shareholders.

Following this, Coca-Cola shows four additional, special components of Shareowners' Equity. *Unearned compensation* refers to the value of stock that has been awarded to certain officers of the company but not yet earned. *Foreign currency translation adjustment* and *Unrealized gain on securities available for sale* represent temporary changes that have occurred in the value of certain assets. Because they are temporary in nature, they aren't immediately recorded as part of the income statement; instead, they are recorded as temporary additions to or subtractions from the value of Shareowners' Equity and are adjusted from period to period until they become permanent or fully realized. Lastly, *Treasury stock* measures amounts that Coca-Cola has paid to reacquire its own stock. Although these shares have not been canceled, they are no longer outstanding and therefore do not represent any owners' interest at the date of the Balance Sheet.

The Statement of Income

The results of operations of business over a period of time are shown in the Statement of Income, or the *Income Statement*. Just as the Balance Sheet can be represented by the accounting equation, the income statement can be represented by the following equation:

$$Revenues \sim Expenses = Net\ Income\ (or\ Net\ Loss)$$

In actual reports, this equation is expanded considerably and usually includes details about the nature of important categories, particularly in footnotes to the statement.

Revenues result from selling products or services to customers. In its Consolidated Statement of Income (see **Exhibit 2**), Coca-Cola shows a single figure for its "Net operating revenues" during the designated periods of time (that is, the years ending December 31, 1996 and 1995). Some companies might give figures for different kinds of revenue.

This is immediately followed by *Cost of goods sold*, which represents, for Coca-Cola, the direct, factory-related cost of producing the products it sold. (If Coca-Cola were a retailer rather than a manufacturer, cost of goods sold would represent the amount of money it paid to outside suppliers for the merchandise that it then resold to the public.) Coca-Cola's *Gross profit* represents simply the difference between Revenues and Cost of goods sold.

Following this is what Coca-Cola labels *Selling, administrative, and general expenses*; other companies sometimes call it *Operating expenses* or will sometimes break it down into a few different categories. This represents general overhead expenses that the company incurred during the designated periods of time. Deducting these general overhead expenses from the Gross profit figure yields the company's *Operating income*, which is thus a measure of the income derived from the principal operations of the company.

The Consolidated Statement of Income of Coca-Cola is typical in that, in addition to operating income, other income and expense items must be added and subtracted before the *net income* total is measured. In many organizations, these nonoperating amounts are significant, but they are shown separately to enable a reader of the financial report to make alternative assumptions about the efficiency and success of operations in the current or future periods.

The Statement of Cash Flows

The *Statement of Cash Flows* details the reasons why the amount of cash (and cash equivalents) changed during an accounting period. Just as the statement of income describes how retained earnings have changed during an accounting period, the statement of cash flows describes how the amount of cash and cash equivalents has changed during the accounting period. The statement's format reflects the three categories of activities that affect cash. Cash can be increased or decreased (1) because of *operations*, (2) because of the acquisition or sale of assets or *investments*, or (3) from changes in debt or stock or other *financial activities*.

Although it may not be self-evident from the Consolidated Statement of Cash Flows from the Coca-Cola Company (see **Exhibit 3**), the statement of cash flows can be thought of as containing much of the same kind of information as a checkbook register or bankbook. Sales or purchases of assets increase or decrease the amount of cash that can be deposited. Borrowing cash or payment of debt affect the balance similarly. Operations have similar effects on the balance of cash available. The reason this analogy to a bank balance is not obvious may be due to the most common form in which the statement of cash flows is presented. This common format reconciles the net income reported in the income statement to the net cash provided by operations. Upon further study, it will become apparent why statements of cash flows are often presented in this format rather than by showing directly the demands for cash made by operations and the receipts of cash provided by operations.

Accounting Concepts

Four basic accounting concepts underlie the presentation in any statement of income. They are the *accounting period concept*, the *accrual concept*, the *realization* or *recognition concept*, and the *matching concept*.

A statement of income is always presented for a period of time. In fact, part of the heading of the statement of income must include a description of the time period for which the income has been measured. The *accounting period concept* covers the period over which a statement of income has been prepared. The accounting period can be of any length, but customarily it is related to a calendar period such as one year, one-half year, or perhaps one month. It is often useful to think of the accounting period as the time between the preparation and presentation of two successive statements of financial position by an organization. The statement of income presents the changes in owners' equity due to operations and other events between one balance sheet and the next.

The *accrual concept* supports the idea that income should be measured at the time major efforts or accomplishments occur rather than simply when cash is received or paid. Revenue and expenses can be recognized before or after cash flows. If revenue is recognized, but cash has not been received, then it will be recorded among current assets as accounts receivable. Correspondingly, if an expense has been incurred, but cash has not been paid, it will be recorded as a current liability.

What accountants call the *realization concept* is really a family of rules that might be more clearly labeled *recognition concepts*. These rules aid the accountant in determining that a revenue or expense has occurred, so that it can be measured, recorded, and reported in financial reports. There is actually a large number of these rules, many of which are conditional on circumstances affecting a particular organization at a particular point in time. For example, revenue is often realized (recognized) when a product is shipped to a customer. However, in other circumstances where a customer has contracted for a special product, some portion of revenue might be recognized at the end of an accounting period, even though the product is not complete and has not been delivered. In general, revenue is recognized along with associated expenses when an exchange has taken place, the earnings process is complete, the amount of income is determinable, and collection of amounts due is reasonably assured.

The amount of expenses to be deducted in each accounting period is determined by the *matching concept* through which the expenses associated with revenue are identified and measured. The accountant attempts to match the cost and expenses of producing a product or service with revenues obtained from its delivery to customers, so that net income can be measured. This matching of revenues and expenses allows readers to understand better the possible expenses of future revenues the organization will try to earn.

Our introduction to the accounting framework and financial reports illustrates four additional accounting concepts. These concepts include the *money measurement concept*, the *business entity concept*, the *going concern concept*, and the *cost concept*.

Accountants measure things in terms of money. The *money measurement concept* has the advantage of expressing all measurements in a common monetary unit that can be added, subtracted, multiplied, and divided to produce reports which themselves can become the subject of further analysis. Nevertheless, there are many things that affect an organization but are difficult or impossible to measure in terms of money. The knowledge and skills of members or employees of an organization have great value, but they are virtually impossible to measure in terms of money. Customer loyalty may ensure future profitability, but only past revenues will be shown in past reports. Because accountants employ the money measurement concept, readers of accounting reports should not expect to find a complete picture or all the facts about an organization.

The *entity concept* delineates the boundaries of the organization for which accounts are kept and reports are made. The reports of the Coca-Cola Company that we have examined contain no information about who the owners or the managers of the Coca-Cola Company are. At the same time, because the accounts of many parts of the Coca-Cola Company have been consolidated, we cannot see the financial condition or financial success of a particular sales office or product line. Common sense tells us that within the Coca-Cola Company, accounts are probably maintained and reports prepared for each of those entities. The entity concept means that anyone who uses financial reports has to be sure that those reports are for the exact entity in which he or she is interested, whether it be the organization as a whole or a particular subset of it.

Financial reports assume that the entity is a *going concern*. Reports are not prepared on a basis that would show the liquidation value of an organization or what would happen if the organization was liquidated. Instead, the accountant works on the assumption that an entity will continue to operate much as it has been operating for an indefinitely long period in the future.

A fourth concept seen in the financial reports you have examined is the *cost concept*. Transactions provide the information necessary for measuring and recording assets in the accounts and subsequently reporting about them. Although a reader of a financial report may be interested in the value of assets or the value of an organization, the accountant is not. Assets are initially recorded by measuring the amount paid for them. When that cost is matched with revenues, it is matched at its historical amount rather than at the current value of the asset used to create a product or service. The cost concept means that as time passes asset measurements are not changed even if the current value of those assets is changing. Likewise, when coupled with the money measurement concept, no allowance is made for changes in the purchasing power of the currency that may have been used to acquire an asset. There can be no doubt that the cost concept greatly simplifies the accountant's job in maintaining a record that can become the basis for financial reports. But it does so by sacrificing the relevance of those reports to many kinds of economic decision making.

Three other concepts are important to financial reporting, even though they are somewhat less obvious. These are the concepts of *conservatism, consistency*, and *materiality*.

The *conservatism concept* operates as a safeguard to overstatement of asset values and owners' equity. It requires that accountants be slower to recognize revenues and gains and quicker to recognize expenses and losses. This potentially negative bias in the accountant's behavior is the basis for many jokes about the differences in the way accountants and other managers see things occurring in organizations.

The *consistency concept* requires that once an entity has selected an accounting method for a kind of event or a particular asset, that same method should be used for all future events of the same type and for that asset. The consistency concept enhances the comparability of accounting reports from one period to that of another. In that way, it enhances the usefulness of financial reports. Nevertheless, certain caution must be attached to any discussion of the consistency concept because accountants use the term consistency in a narrower sense than found in other uses. Consistency is required all the time, but there is no requirement for logical consistency at a moment in time. For example, assets that may appear identical may be accounted for using different accounting methods. All that is required is that the same method be used for the same asset over time, not that all like assets be accounted for using the same method. This means that financial statement users must be constantly alert for the specific accounting methods used in different parts of financial reports. Just because a reader of financial reports understands the way in which factory machinery has been measured and reported does not necessarily mean that the same reader will have any idea how trucks or delivery equipment have been measured and reported.

Finally, arching over the entire process of accounting and financial reporting is the *materiality concept*. This concept allows that the accountant does not need to attempt to measure and record events that are insignificant or to highlight events that differ from the usual or the norm. Events or assets judged to be insignificant can be ignored or disregarded. On the surface, this concept would seem to make good sense, as it focuses both the accountant and the financial report reader's attention on important things. Unfortunately, the exact line between what is significant and what is insignificant is very difficult to define. Furthermore, something may seem insignificant to the accountant but might be regarded as very significant to a managing director. The materiality concept is both a strength and a weakness in financial reporting, and a wise reader of reports must be constantly on guard for its occasionally pernicious effects.

Summary

The accounting equation

$$Assets = Equities$$

or in its expanded form

$$Assets = Liabilities + Owners' Equity$$

Assets − Liabilities = Owners' Equity

provides the basis for the accounting framework. The format for the statement of financial position derives directly from the accounting equation, and the assumed equality of assets and equities provides a basis for accounting record systems as well as the statement of financial position.

Two additional financial reports stem directly from the accounting equation. The statement of income explains the change in the owners' equity that occurs during an accounting period by giving details of both revenues that increase owners' equity and expenses that decrease owners' equity. It provides a basis for analyzing the effectiveness of operations. The statement of cash flows explains why the amount of cash and equivalents has increased or decreased during a period of time. It details whether or not operations have provided additional cash or have themselves consumed cash. It also reveals cash that is provided by new loans or that has been used to pay off debts, and how cash has been invested or obtained by selling assets.

This brief overview of the accounting framework and financial reporting has served as an introduction to eleven important accounting concepts, financial reports, and the work of accountants. Only practice and further study can give real meaning to these accounting concepts, but understanding their existence is critical to studying the work of accountants, and some of the reasons why they operate as they do. The 11 concepts introduced here include: accounting period, accrual, realization, matching, money measurement, entity, going concern, cost, consistency, conservatism, and materiality. We will see in detail how these concepts are applied as we continue in our study of accounting principles.

Exhibit 1 The Coca-Cola Company and Subsidiaries—Consolidated Balance Sheet (in millions except share data)

December 31	1996	1995
ASSETS		
Current		
Cash and cash equivalents	$ 1,433	$ 1,167
Marketable securities	225	148
	1,658	1,315
Trade accounts receivable, less allowance of $30 in 1996 and $34 in 1995	1,641	1,695
Inventories	952	1,117
Prepaid expenses and other assets	1,659	1,323
Total Current Assets	5,910	5,450
Investments and Other Assets		
Equity method investments:		
Coca-Cola Enterprises, Inc.	547	556
Cocal-Cola Amatil Limited	881	682
Other, principally bottling companies	2,004	1,157
Cost method investments, principally bottling companies	737	319
Marketable securities and other assets	1,779	1,597
	5,948	4,311
Property, Plant and Equipment		
Land	204	233
Buildings and improvements	1,528	1,944
Machinery and equipment	3,649	4,135
Containers	200	345
	5,581	6,657
Less allowances for depreciation	2,031	2,321
	3,550	4,336
Goodwill and Other Intangible Assets	753	944
	$16,161	$15,041

Exhibit 1 (continued)   The Coca-Cola Company and Subsidiaries—Consolidated Balance Sheet (in millions except share data)

December 31	1996	1995
LIABILITIES AND SHAREOWNERS' EQUITY		
Current		
Accounts payable and accrued expenses	$ 2,972	$ 3,103
Loans and notes payable	3,388	2,371
Current maturities of long-term debt	9	552
Accrued income taxes	1,037	1,322
Total Current Liabilities	7,406	7,348
Long-term Debt	1,116	1,141
Other Liabilities	1,182	966
Deferred Income Taxes	301	194
Shareowners' Equity		
Common stock, $.25 par value		
Authorized: 5,600,000,000 shares		
Issued: 3,432,956,518 shares in 1996; 3,423,678,994 in 1995	858	856
Capital surplus	1,058	863
Reinvested earnings	15,127	12,882
Unearned compensation related to outstanding restricted stock	(61)	(68)
Foreign currency translation adjustment	(662)	(424)
Unrealized gain on securities available for sale	156	82
	16,476	14,191
Less treasury stock, at cost (951,963,574 shares in 1996; 919,081,326 shares in 1995)	10,320	8,799
	6,156	5,392
	$16,161	$15,041

Exhibit 2 The Coca-Cola Company and Subsidiaries—Consolidated Statement of Income (in millions, except per share data)

Year Ended December 31	1996	1995	1994
Net Operating Revenues	$18,546	$18,018	$16,181
Cost of goods sold	6,738	6,940	6,168
Gross Profit	11,808	11,078	10,013
Selling, administrative, and general expenses	7,893	7,052	6,376
Operating Income	3,915	4,026	3,637
Interest income	238	245	181
Interest expense *debt obligation*	286	272	199
Equity income	211	169	134
Other income (deductions)—net	87	86	(25)
Gains on issuances of stock by equity investees	431	74	--
Income before Income Taxes	4,596	4,328	3,728
Income taxes	1,104	1,342	1,174
Net Income	$ 3,492	$ 2,986	$ 2,554
Net Income per Share	$ 1.40	$ 1.18	$ .99
Average Shares Outstanding	2,494	2,525	2,580

Exhibit 3   The Coca-Cola Company and Subsidiaries—Consolidated Statement of Cash Flows (in millions)

Year Ended December 31	1996	1995	1994
Operating Activities			
Net income	$3,492	$ 2,986	$2,554
Depreciation and amortization	479	454	411
Deferred income taxes	(145)	157	58
Equity income, net of dividends	(89)	(25)	(4)
Foreign currency adjustments	(60)	(23)	(6)
Gains on issuances of stock by equity investees	(431)	(74)	--
Other noncash items	181	45	41
Net change in operating assets and liabilities	36	(192)	307
Net cash provided by operating activities	3,463	3,328	3,361
Investing Activities			
Acquisitions and investments, principally bottling companies	(645)	(338)	(311)
Purchases of investments and other assets	(623)	(403)	(379)
Proceeds from disposals of investments and other assets	1,302	580	299
Purchases of property, plant, and equipment	(990)	(937)	(878)
Proceeds from disposals of property, plant, and equipment	81	44	109
Other investing activities	(175)	(172)	(55)
Net cash used in investing activities	(1,050)	(1,226)	(1,215)
Net cash provided by operations after reinvestment	2,413	2,102	2,146
Financing Activities			
Issuances of debt	1,112	754	491
Payments of debt	(580)	(212)	(154)
Issuances of stock	124	86	69
Purchases of stock for treasury	(1,521)	(1,796)	(1,192)
Dividends	(1,247)	(1,110)	(1,006)
Net cash used in financing activities	(2,102)	(2,278)	(1,792)
Effect of Exchange Rate Changes on Cash and Cash Equivalents	(45)	(43)	34
Cash and Cash Equivalents			
Net increase (decrease) during the year	266	(219)	388
Balance at beginning of year	1,167	1,386	998
Balance at end of year	$1,433	$1,167	$1,386

RECOGNIZING REVENUES AND EXPENSES: REALIZED AND EARNED

(R.S. Kaplan / #9-100-050 / 5 p)

Summary

Describes a key concept in financial accounting: choosing an appropriate revenue recognition point. The accrual process requires revenue recognition and expense matching for reporting on the value creation process of companies. Describes the two key criteria for revenue recognition – realized and earned – and the conditions that must be met to satisfy these criteria. The use of the typical recognition point, when the product or service is delivered to the customer, is discussed as well as situations (e.g., the percentage-of-completion method) when revenue can be recognized before actual delivery.

Outline

When Should Revenues be Recognized?

Applying the Revenue Recognition Rule

Measuring Revenue Prior to Delivery

Applying the Matching Concept

A Final Comment

Learning Objectives

After reading the note and completing the following exercises, managers should be able to:

- Grasp the basic criteria for recognizing revenues.

- Better understand how their firm recognizes revenues, and why that approach is used.

Questions and Ideas to Consider

1. Consider the products or services your company offers, and how it offers them. Is it a fairly simple matter to recognize revenues from these products or services? What might delay recognition of revenue?

2. Review the five common revenue recognition points in the "Timing of revenue recognition" section. At which point does your firm recognize revenues for its products and services? In general, does your firm take a liberal or conservative approach to recognizing revenue? What are the advantages and disadvantages of this approach?

Recognizing Revenues and Expenses: Realized and Earned

Companies create value continually. Manufacturing companies purchase materials and pay employees to convert raw materials and purchased parts into intermediate and finished goods. At the same time, other employees, in marketing and sales, are working to generate orders from customers. Manufacturing efforts culminate with producing a completed, finished product. Marketing and sales efforts culminate with obtaining a customer order. When both events have occurred, the company can ship the finished product to the customer. Sometime later, the customer pays the company for the product. This process continually repeats: purchasing materials, producing finished products, generating orders, shipping products to customers, and collecting payments.

In an ideal world, the accounting statements would report increases in value continually as the company performs the following steps (not necessarily in the sequence shown) in its operating cycle:

- acquires the materials it needs to produce products

- processes materials and parts through successive production stages

- generates customer orders

- ships products to customers

- invoices customers for products and services, and

- collects cash from customers.

In practice, of course, such continual recognition of value creation is infeasible.

Accountants generally choose one date when all (or a significant portion of) the cash receipts are *recognized* as revenues and *matched* with all the expenses (the cash expenditures) associated with generating the revenues. The *realization concept* underlies the decision rules that accountants use to determine when revenues should be recognized and expenses matched to them. The *matching concept*

Professor Robert S. Kaplan adapted this note from one originally authored by Professor William J. Bruns, Jr. to facilitate class discussion.

relates revenues and expenses so that the income (increase in value to the company) from the event can be reliably estimated.

Questions about the time at which revenue should be measured and recognized in reports are not always easy to answer, particularly if the accountant seeks to provide reliable and verifiable information. At first glance, the easy answer would be to recognize revenue only when cash is received. Recognizing and measuring revenues when cash is received constitute the *cash basis for accounting*. Using the cash basis, expenses are recognized when cash is expended; this would typically be much earlier than when the cash is received for delivering the product or service.

The only reason for considering use of the cash basis for accounting for revenues and expenses is simplicity. By counting cash received, revenues can be easily measured. By counting cash spent, expenses are easily measured. But cash is only one of the resources that most organizations employ in carrying out operations and seeking to enhance the wealth of owners.

The alternative to the cash basis occurs when revenues are recognized and measured on the *accrual basis*. The accrual basis is usually assumed to provide better information to owners on the results of operations and better information to those who use information from financial reports in making decisions. Under the accrual basis, accountants may recognize revenues when delivery of product or service has occurred even if cash has not yet been received. Under the accrual basis, expenses will also be measured and recognized in the same accounting period as the revenues to which they relate.

The advantages of cash accounting need not be completely lost when the accrual basis is used. A summary of the monetary transactions of an organization or a statement of cash flows can easily be prepared to supplement balance sheets and income statements prepared on an accrual basis. Because no information is lost, and because there appear to be important reasons to favor use the accrual basis for calculating income, the accrual basis has become the standard used by companies to measure and recognize revenues, expenses, and income.

When Should Revenues by Recognized?

Recognition of revenue in a period requires that two criteria be satisfied:

1. The revenue is *realized*, or realizable

2. The revenue is *earned*

We discuss the conditions that must be satisfied for revenue to be realized and earned.

1. The *realization* criterion is satisfied when all three of the following conditions occur:

    i.   The revenue–the amount the customers will pay–can be objectively measured

    ii. The eventual collection of cash (or cash-equivalents) can be reasonably assured

    iii. Any remaining fulfillment costs can be estimated with reasonable reliability and accuracy.

The first condition requires that the terms of the agreement are clear to both sides and that the amount to be paid for the product or service can be estimated with a tolerable margin of error. In general, accountants want to have confidence that the amount to be received is verifiable, reliable, and free from undue management bias. Some amount of uncertainty in the amount to be owed can be tolerated. If, however, the uncertainty of the sale price is too great, then revenue recognition may be deferred until such uncertainty can be reduced.

The second condition requires evidence that the customer both expects to pay and is able to pay. For example, in purchasing land through monthly installments paid over a ten-year period, the company may wait until a customer has made 10 or 20 payments before recognizing the full sales price for the land. When only one or two payments have been made, customers may reconsider their decisions and decide to forfeit ownership rights by not making any further payments. But to wait until all 120 payments (12 payments per year for 10 years) have been made to recognize the income from the transaction will make financial statements less timely and useful for investors.

The third condition allows for the possibility that the company may incur additional costs even after the revenue recognition point as part of the sale. The most common example is when a company offers a warranty on a product. Rather than wait until the warranty has expired to recognize revenue on the sale, the company may recognize the sale in the period when the product transfers ownership. In this case, the company must also estimate its future warranty costs and match these estimated expenses with the revenue from the sale.

2.   The *earned* criterion is satisfied when the two following conditions have been satisfied:

> i.   The company has completed a substantial portion of the production and sales effort
>
> ii. The risks of ownership have been shifted to the customer

Using the first condition, even when a company has received cash for a product or service–such as when a magazine publisher receives a subscription and cash from a customer–it does not recognize revenue. The publisher has accomplished its sales effort by getting the subscription, but it has yet to perform the major production effort of writing, editing, and producing a monthly magazine and shipping it to the customer. Similarly, if a company has completed a major portion of its production effort, by producing an item for its finished goods inventory, it does not recognize revenue until a customer's order is received (the substantial portion of the sales effort) and the item is shipped to the customer.

The second condition, risk- of- ownership, may be violated when a company ships an item to a customer, but the customer can easily return the item for a refund. For example, book publishers often ship their products to retailers on consignment. The retailer may pay only when the books are sold to end-use consumers, or reserves the right to ship unsold books back to the publishers. In these circumstances, the publisher would not have earned the revenue until its book has been sold to the end-use consumer. Thus the recognition point would occur later than the time when the product has been shipped to the retailer, the publisher's immediate customer.

Timing of revenue recognition

Applying the principles of realized and earned in practice leads to a surprising diversity of points when revenue may be recognized as a result of sale of goods or services to customers. Five of the most common possibilities are:

1. The point at which an order is obtained from a customer.

2. The point at which an order is accepted and the terms of the sale are finalized.

3. The point at which goods are delivered to a customer.

4. The point at which the customer is billed.

5. The point at which payment is received from the customer.

Managers, especially those in marketing and sales, often want to recognize revenue as early as possible in the value-creation cycle, such as at point 1 or point 2 above. Accountants, being more conservative, prefer a later time for recognition such as point 3, or point 4, or perhaps even some later point in time such as point 5. At those points, the accountants believe, an observable market exchange has occurred that satisfies the earned and realized criteria. In most cases, generally accepted accounting principles call for revenues to be recognized at the time goods or services are delivered to the customer. Depending upon the legal form of the sales contract, delivery can take place when goods or services are shipped by the seller or when they are received by the buyer. This is the earliest point at which an outsider can independently determine that a sale has been completed. At that point in time, most critical earnings events have taken place, and the pragmatic issues of probable collection of receivables can be addressed.

Applying the Revenue Recognition Rule

One advantage of using the rule that revenue should be recognized when goods or services are delivered is that recognizing revenue at that time is fairly simple. When a customer buys goods in a retail store and carries the goods out the door, it is clear that something has happened and easy to see that a sale has been completed. In many other cases, as well, where goods or services are delivered to customers, the events can be observed, and the earned and realized criteria can be satisfied. The ease of applying the rule for recognizing revenue at the time of delivery does not mean, however, that there are not important judgments to be made by managers and accountants about revenue recognition. Some of these judgments involve deciding how much revenue should be recognized, and others stem from other events that might take place. What, for example, should be done if merchandise is returned? What if additional services are required to satisfy the customer?

Since it is inevitable that some merchandise will be returned for credit, the amount actually reported as revenue frequently is reduced by estimated or actual returns for credit or refund, or for discounts that have been offered for prompt payment. Thus, it is not uncommon for the first line of an income statement to be labeled *net sales*. If there are important timing differences between the delivery of merchandise and the time it is returned or cash discounts taken, allowances for returns and discounts may be established as accounts and may appear in the statement of financial position as liabilities.

Measuring Revenue Prior to Delivery

Sometimes recognizing revenue on delivery does not provide the best information concerning actual events. One example is when an item is created or manufactured over a long period of time under contract to a customer. Large buildings, ships, and special production facilities designed and constructed as a special order for a customer are examples of items that may take several accounting periods to complete. The entire effort of an organization may be spent working for several periods completing one item. In these cases, deferring recognition of income until the contract work is completely satisfied and the customer accepts the finished outcome does not give readers of financial reports an adequate sense of the value being continually created by the company.

When the production cycle is long and involves large items, and where the income pattern of the firm will be distorted by deferring all recognition of revenue and hence all income to the period of delivery, accountants use procedures by which some of the anticipated income from a project can be recognized as project milestones have been completed. Using the *percentage-of-completion method*, a portion of the total revenue on a project is recognized in each period over the life of the project, and an appropriate amount of expenses is matched to it. [As an exercise, students should think about the situation that enables all five conditions for realized and earned to be satisfied when using the percentage-of-completion method.]

Revenue recognition before the time of delivery may also occur when product prices are determined in well-established public markets. Precious metals, grains and other agricultural products, have readily determinable prices and can often be sold without significant effort. In this situation, revenues can be recognized when the production process has been completed and the product has become available for delivery and sale. This case is perfectly consistent with the earned and realized revenue recognition criteria specified earlier. First, the major economic event has occurred with the production of the product or extraction of the mineral. Second, no significant sales effort is required to sell the product in the market at a known and easily verifiable price.

Applying the Matching Concept

Once revenues have been recognized, the cost of creating the goods and services that were sold are matched to the revenues. Many times there is a fairly obvious and straightforward relationship between expenditures that have been made to create the revenue-producing process and the revenues themselves. In other situations, such as expenditures for advertising or research and development, the relationship between expenditures and revenues is less clear, and expenditures for these efforts will be matched to revenues in the period in which the expenditure takes place.

Finally, there is a kind of expense that can be difficult to observe, measure, and recognize. These are commitments that arise from promises of future expenditures, beyond the period in which revenues have been earned. Warranties or commitments to employees for pensions or other post-retirement benefits are examples of this kind of promise. In these cases, past transactions do not provide information about the amount of expense. Instead, estimates of the amount of future expenses must be made so that the current expenses matched with the revenues will include all the expenses associated with the revenue-generating event.

A Final Comment

Revenue recognition can generate heated conflicts between managers and accountants. Most everyone in an organization wants to recognize organizational success quickly. Accounting criteria for revenue recognition–realized and earned–and an underlying accounting philosophy of conservatism operate as checks on early revenue recognition. Everyone in an organization may be thrilled when a large contract is signed or a big order from an important customer is received. They are sure that the value of the organization has been enhanced. But until the products and services promised under the contract have been delivered to customers, or the criteria for the percentage of completion process have been met, no revenue–and hence, no income–can be reported.

ACCOUNTING FOR CURRENT ASSETS

(W.J. Bruns, Jr. / #9-193-048 / 10 p)

Summary

An introduction to accounting for current assets: receivables, inventories, and other current assets. Included are discussions of FIFO, LIFO, average cost, and explanation of accounting for manufactured inventories.

Outline

Cash, Cash Equivalents, and Other Temporary Investments

Accounts Receivable

Inventories

Accounting for Manufactured Inventories

Other Current Assets

Learning Objectives

After reading the note and completing the following exercises, managers should be able to:

- Become familiar with the basic categories of current assets on their firm's balance sheet.

- Understand how inventories – raw materials, work in process, and finished goods – are accounted for throughout the manufacturing process.

- Understand the three methods of measuring inventory cost flows and why one might be used rather than another.

Questions and Ideas to Consider

1. Which method (average cost, FIFO, or LIFO) does your company use to account for inventory cost? Why do you think this particular method is used?

2. Consider the work done by your department or unit. How does your unit impact product costs? At what point does it intersect the inventory cost flow? In other words, does your unit:

   - purchase raw materials?
   - manufacture or assemble part of the finished product?
   - provide a service connected with the production of inventory?

You might use Exhibit 3 as a guide to understanding where your unit is involved.

Accounting For Current Assets

Current assets are those resources that are expected to benefit the organization within the next operating cycle. Current assets reported by the Gillette Company and Subsidiary Companies in their 1995 Annual Report are typical (see **Exhibit 1**). *Cash and cash equivalents* and *short-term investments* always head the list of current assets, and they are the means by which current operating expenses can be met. Other current assets are usually listed in an order that approximates their nearness to cash; *inventories* are available for sale to customers, whose accounts then become *accounts receivable*, which when paid become cash to replenish the inventory pool to start the cycle again. These flows are going on continuously, and the balance sheet merely provides a view at one moment in time.

Cash, Cash Equivalents, and Other Temporary Investments

The title *Cash and Cash Equivalents* has become very prevalent as more and more organizations engage in cash management techniques. Since idle cash provides no return, financial managers try to invest any temporary excess amounts of cash in highly liquid, short-term investments. Money market funds, government securities, certificates of deposit, or high-grade commercial paper are some of the investments that may be used for this purpose. Because they can be readily resold and converted into cash, accounting treats them as if they are cash.

Forecasting cash receipts and disbursements is an important part of the treasury function in most corporations. Since the yield (interest earned) on investments tends to be higher on marketable securities that are less liquid, many organizations invest a part of their excess cash in other marketable securities, which are shown separately as temporary investments. For most purposes, the distinction between cash equivalents and other temporary investments in marketable securities is unimportant, except as an indication of the investment horizon in a cash management program.

Accounts Receivable

When a sale to a customer is made on terms other than cash, an account receivable is created. Accounts receivable from customers are reported at the amount that is expected to be received from customers in settlement of their obligations. This may differ from the total of stated selling prices for two reasons. First, as an inducement for prompt payment, customers may be offered a *cash discount* if they pay within a short period of time. Second, although there is an assumption at the time of every sale that customers will pay, in practice not all do. For this reason, a valuation adjustment, or *allowance for*

Professor William J. Bruns, Jr., prepared this note as the basis for class discussion rather than to illustrate either effective or ineffective handling of an administrative situation.

doubtful accounts, is normally recorded to recognize that some accounts will become *bad debts* and to bring the accounts receivable balance to a more realistic level.

Cash discounts are normally anticipated at the time of sale and deducted from sales, creating an allowance for cash discounts that is deducted from the total amount owed by customers to arrive at the amount of accounts receivable included in the balance sheet. The amount of the allowance is almost always based on the company's past experience with cash discounts taken by customers.

The problem in estimating the amounts that customers will not pay (bad debts) is somewhat more complex. Most organizations know from experience that some customers will be unable or unwilling to pay the amounts they owe. The problem is that at the time a sale is made and a receivable is recorded, managers do not know which customers will pay and which will not. The solution to this problem lies in making an estimate that is based on past experience of the portion of accounts receivable that will not be paid in full either at the time it is due or within some reasonable time thereafter.

A number of methods are used to estimate the *allowance for doubtful accounts*, also called the *allowance for bad debts*. Sometimes a percentage of the total amount of sales is charged to expense during the period in which sales are made, and that amount is established as an allowance against which bad accounts are offset when they are finally identified. The percentage of sales taken is customarily based on the experience of the firm with its particular group of customers, and it may vary with the type of customer to which sales are made.

Alternatively, an examination could be made of the distribution of accounts according to how long they have been outstanding. The percentage used to estimate default on accounts already overdue can be different from that applied to accounts that have not reached the point where payment is expected. Estimating the amount of accounts that will not be collected is an important aspect of reporting realistic figures for accounts receivable. If no allowance for doubtful accounts is made, the amount of accounts receivable may be overstated.

Inventories

Inventories are considered a significant current asset in many firms. By holding an inventory of finished product, an organization can fill orders more quickly and provide better customer service. Even when products or services have to be created after a customer order is received, inventories of raw materials speed the process of satisfying customer demands.

Accounting for inventories has two important aspects. First, the cost of inventory that is purchased or manufactured has to be determined. That cost is then held in the inventory accounts of the firm until the product is sold. Once the product has been shipped or delivered to a customer, the cost becomes an expense to be reported in the income statement as the cost of goods sold.

To understand the process of inventory accounting, you have to imagine costs flowing into the inventory account and then being removed from that account and charged to cost of goods sold in the income statement. Just as products are physically moved onto shelves or into a warehouse and then physically removed as they are delivered to customers, so too is the cost of inventory moved into an account and later removed from it. It is important to recognize, however, that the flows need not be parallel, that is, the flow of costs into and out of the inventory account need not be in the same order as the flow of goods into and out of the warehouse.

Inventory Cost Flows

At first glance, it seems there is no need to make an assumption about how costs flow through the inventory account. The cost of each item placed in the physical inventory can be entered into the account, and then, as the item is physically taken from inventory, the cost can be removed from the account. In this way, the costs accumulated in the account can match perfectly with the items physically held, and the costs of goods sold can be equal to the sum of the cost of each item actually delivered to a customer. Such an inventory cost system can be identified as a *specific identification* system.

Specifically identifying each item in inventory is relatively easy if each item is unique, such as an art object, expensive jewelry, or custom-made furniture, or if each item has an identification number, such as an automobile. However, specific identification is not practical for a company having a large number of inventory items that are not easily identifiable individually. In these cases, it is common for accountants to assume a flow of cost through the inventory account that is unrelated in any way to the actual physical flow of goods.

Three common assumptions used in accounting for inventory cost are: (1) average cost, (2) first-in, first-out (FIFO), and (3) last-in, first-out (LIFO). A company can choose any of these three assumptions and use them consistently for each classification of inventory regardless of the way in which goods physically move into and out of inventory.

Using the *average-cost method* requires calculation of the average cost of items in the beginning inventory plus purchases made during the accounting period to determine the cost of goods sold and the cost of inventory on hand at the end of the period. The average cost is assumed to be a representative cost of all the items available for sale during the accounting period. Rather than wait until the end of an accounting period to calculate the average cost, some companies use a predetermined unit cost of all transactions that take place during the accounting period. This is a *standard-cost system* and is a variation of the average-cost method. Any difference between the actual average unit cost and the predetermined standard cost during a period is usually added to or subtracted from the cost of goods sold for that period.

If the *first-in first-out*, or *FIFO*, assumption is used, the oldest costs in the inventory account are the first to be transferred to cost of goods sold when merchandise is sold. Using this assumption means that the costs retained in the inventory account will always be those most recently incurred for the purchase or manufacture of inventory. For this reason, the FIFO assumption produces an inventory account balance that usually comes the closest of the three methods to approximating the replacement cost of the inventory.

The *last-in first-out*, or *LIFO*, assumption is the opposite of FIFO. Cost of goods sold is measured using the cost of the most recent additions to inventory, and the inventory account always retains the oldest cost of items purchased or manufactured. *This assumed cost flow may be quite different from the actual physical flow of goods, and it usually is when the LIFO method is used.* If older costs are retained in the inventory account for some time because the inventory is never depleted, and if prices change substantially in the accounting periods during which these old costs are retained, the LIFO inventory balance will likely bear little relation to the current value of the same amount of inventory recently purchased.

Use of the LIFO assumption is not permitted in some countries. It is, however, permitted in the United States and is quite popular. The reasons for this popularity are rooted in the fact that the United States has experienced fairly continuous inflation and cost increases for many commodities and goods. Since the LIFO assumption can be used in reporting income for income taxation purposes, firms choose to use it to reduce income taxes that are due in the current period. For most accounting methods, there is no requirement under U.S. tax law that the same method be employed in financial reports issued to shareholders and in financial reports on which taxes are based. However, LIFO is an exception. A company that chooses to save taxes by using the LIFO assumption must also use the LIFO method in its reports to shareholders. For this reason, the cost associated with paying lower taxes comes from the fact that management must then report to shareholders lower earnings than might be the case if an alternative inventory assumption were used.

These three common assumptions–average cost, LIFO, and FIFO–are illustrated in **Exhibit 2**. The differences caused by the differing flow assumptions are a function of the rate at which prices have changed during the period as well as the length of time old costs have been retained in the account because of the LIFO assumption. The important thing to remember is that the inventory cost flow assumption has an impact on cost of goods sold, reported net income, and the inventory value that will be shown among the current assets in the statement of financial position. The amount of difference between cost of goods sold reported under one assumption and cost of goods sold reported under another will depend on the speed with which costs of inventory are changing.

A reader of financial reports also has to be alert for situations in which the LIFO assumption has been used and inventory costs acquired many periods beforehand have been allowed to flow into cost of goods sold. Assuming the costs of inventory have risen, dipping into these old inventory costs by reducing the size of inventory on hand (called a LIFO liquidation) will give a burst of net income, which may not be sustainable in future periods.

We can sum up our discussion of inventory accounting to this point quite simply. Inventory accounting consists of measuring the cost of items that are added to inventory and then choosing the flow assumption to determine which of those costs are moved first to cost of goods sold when inventory is sold and delivered to customers. In organizations that only purchase items for their own use or for resale to others, the only other issue that arises is whether a perpetual record of inventory purchases and deliveries is kept or whether the firm relies on a periodic inventory count to determine the quantity of inventory on hand at the end of an accounting period that will be carried forward as the beginning inventory in the subsequent period. However, many organizations buy materials, expend labor on changing their character, and manufacture products or create services, which all add cost to the products eventually delivered to customers. These firms require additional records and account classifications in order to record and report properly their inventories.

Accounting for Manufactured Inventories

The record keeping required to maintain control of inventory items as their form and character change is often complex and voluminous. A branch of accounting known as *cost accounting* is devoted to analysis and study of the type of problems encountered in measuring and recording information necessary to determine the cost of inventories and the effects of expenditures and expenses incurred during the manufacturing process.

In the case of manufactured inventory, it is necessary to choose a flow assumption just as we would in a case where inventory was only purchased and sold. Since inventories are typically in several different forms in the manufacturing firm—raw materials, work in process, and finished goods—the record-keeping task is necessarily more complex. Labor and supplies may be used to alter raw materials, increasing the amount and cost of work in process. Raw materials and labor may be necessary to create finished goods. Costs now flow not only within classifications of the inventory according to assumptions (FIFO, LIFO and so on), but the amount used becomes the input for another class of inventory. In a typical manufacturing firm, the flow is like that depicted in **Exhibit 3**. **Exhibit 4** is a numerical illustration of the way in which costs might be assumed to flow through the inventory accounts in a simple manufacturing company. **Exhibit 5** shows how the cost of goods sold can be detailed in a comprehensive statement of income for the same firm.

Although the application of particular flow assumptions used in the manufacturing firm demands care (and occasionally ingenuity) on the part of the accountant, the problems of inventory accounting are essentially the same in all organizations. As inventories become a relatively larger portion of the total working capital or total assets of a firm, issues of inventory costing and measurement become more and more important and demand more attention of management.

Other Current Assets

The major category of other current assets that you are likely to encounter in financial reports is *prepaid expenses*. In most cases, these are expenditures that have not yet become expenses because they have future value to the firm. They will be matched with revenue in subsequent accounting periods as their usefulness has been realized. Typical examples might be rents paid in advance for machinery or facilities that will be used in future months, amounts paid as insurance premiums at the beginning of insurance coverage, and travel-expense advances to employees for trips to be subsequently taken. These deferred expenses are typically used up over a short period of time, and for this reason, they are classified as current assets.

Summary

Because the items classified as current assets are so important to current operations, they tend to turn over fairly quickly. The amounts shown on the balance sheet are usually fairly close to the amount that would be paid for a replacement asset of the same classification. The major exception to this is the inventory account during periods of rapid price changes, or if the LIFO inventory flow assumption is used.

In most organizations, there is a logical flow through those assets reported as current assets. Cash is used to purchase or create inventory. Inventory is delivered to customers, and their accounts become receivables. Receivables are collected, making cash available for operations. This flow is what operations are about. These operating assets are what demand management's day-to-day attention as inventories are turned into more liquid assets to finance the creation of more inventories ready to satisfy customer orders.

Exhibit 1   Current Assets, The Gillette Company and Subsidiary Companies (Except from
Consolidated Balance Sheets) ($ millions)

Current Assets	December 31, 1995	December 31, 1994
Cash and cash equivalents	$47.9	$43.8
Short-term investments, at cost which approximates market	1.6	2.3
Receivable less allowances: 1995-$59.2; 1994-$52.1	1,659.5	1,379.5
Inventories	1,035.1	941.2
Deferred income taxes	220.2	220.6
Prepaid expenses	140.2	113.0
Total Current Assets	$3,104.5	$2,700.4

Notes to Consolidated Financial Statements

Cash and Cash Equivalents

Cash and cash equivalents include cash, time deposits and all highly liquid debt instruments with an original maturity of three months or less.

Inventories

(Millions of dollars)	December 31. 1995	December 31, 1994
Raw materials and supplies	$231.8	$207.3
Work in process	127.3	95.0
Finished goods	676.0	638.9
	$1,035.1	$941.2

Inventories are stated at the lower of cost or market. In general, cost is currently adjusted standard cost, which approximates actual cost on a first-in, first-out basis.

Income Taxes

Beginning in 1993, deferred taxes are provided for using the asset and liability method for temporary differences between financial and tax reporting.

Exhibit 2   Inventory Cost-Flow Assumptions Illustrated

The Xitan Plumbing Supply Company maintained an inventory of standard brass faucets for sale to plumbers. In 1992, because of increasing copper prices, the price paid to suppliers increased significantly. A record of purchases in 1992 showed the following:

February 1	50 @ $ 6.00	$ 300
April 1	50 @ 7.50	375
May 1	50 @ 8.50	425
July 1	50 @ 9.00	450
October 1	50 @ 10.50	525
		$2,075

Prices had been stable prior to 1992. On January 1, 1992, there were 29 faucets on hand, each of which had cost $5.00. At the end of the year on December 31, there were 54 faucets on hand.

If inventories are valued periodically, the value of inventory in terms of historical prices and the cost of faucets sold depends on the inventory flow assumption adopted, as shown below:

Xitan Plumbing Supply Company—Expense Standard Brass Faucets—1992

	Assumed Flow of Costs		
	First-in, First-Out	**Average Cost**	**Last-in, First-Out**
Brass faucets, January 1, 1992 29 @ $5.00	$ 145	$ 145	$ 145
Purchases, 1992	2,075	2,075	2,075
Available for sale, 1992	$2,220	$2,220	$2,220
Brass faucets, December 31, 1992 FIFO: 50 @ $10.50 = $525 4 @ 9.00 = 36	561		
Average cost: 54 @ $7.96[a]		430	
LIFO: 29 @ $5.00 = $145 25 @ 6.00 = 150			561
			295
Cost of faucets sold, 1992	$1,659	$1,790	$1,925

[a]Average cost is measured here by taking the total cost of brass faucets purchased and dividing it by the total number of faucets purchased.

Exhibit 3   Inventory Flows in Manufacturing

1. Materials and parts are purchased for use in manufacturing

Raw Materials at Beginning of Period

 + Purchases

 - To work in process

2. Cost flow of raw materials into manufacturing processes is assumed as labor and other costs are assumed to add to value

Work in Process at Beginning of Period

  + Raw materials used

  + Cost of labor

  + Other manufacturing costs (cost of management; heat, power, and light; supplies used; depreciation

  - To finished goods

3. Cost flow of goods finished is assumed as products are completed and ready for sale

Finished Goods at Beginning of Period

  + Goods completed

  + Goods purchased ready for sale

  - Cost of products sold

Exhibit 4   Manufactured Inventory Accounting Illustrated

The Astroweld Company produces and distributes an advanced technology home welding unit. From two suppliers, the company purchases two parts assemblies—one electrical and one mechanical— for each finished welding unit. These are assembled by company employees using company-owned equipment in a rented factory building. The firm uses *LIFO* flow assumptions for all inventories except work in process.

During May of last year these inventory accounts showed the following conditions and events:

Raw Materials—Electrical Parts Assemblies		
On hand, May 1	15 @ $33	$ 495
May purchases	10 @ $39	390
		$ 885
On hand, May 31	13 @ $33	429
May usage (10 @ $39, 2 @ $33)	12	$ 456
Raw Materials—Mechanical Parts Assemblies		
On hand, May 1	19 @ $10	$ 190
May purchases	10 @ $11	110
		$ 300
On hand, May 31	14 @ $10	140
May usage (10 @ $11, 5 @ $10)	15	$ 160
Manufacturing Costs for May		
Assembly labor		$ 650
Supervisory salaries		220
Heat, light, and power		56
Depreciation of equipment		120
Supplies used		32
Total		$1,078
Work in Process		
In process, May 1		None
Processing in May		
12 electrical parts	$ 456	
15 mechanical parts	160	
Manufacturing costs	1,078	
		$1,694
In process, May 31		
3 mechanical parts (3 @ $10)	$ 30	
Labor cost	40	
Cost of supervision	10	
		80
Transferred to finished goods in May		$1,614
Finished Welders		
On hand, May 1 5 @ $127.50		$ 637.50
May production from work in process		1,614.00
On hand, May 31 2 @ $127.50		(255.00)
Cost of welders sold in May		$1,996.50

Since 12 welders were completed in May and transferred to finished goods at a total cost of $1,614, the average cost of each welder manufactured was $134.50.

An income statement for May for Astroweld might show expense of goods sold as shown in **Exhibit 5**.

Exhibit 5   Astroweld Company—Cost of Welders Sold—May

Raw Materials Cost			
Raw materials–electrical, May 1	$495.00		
Purchases	390.00		
Total available	$885.00		
Raw materials—electrical, May 31	429.00		
To work in process		$ 456.00	
Raw materials—mechanical, May 1	$190.00		
Purchases	110.00		
Total available	$300.00		
Raw materials–mechanical, May 31	140.00		
To work in process		160.00	
Work in process, May 1		0	
Add: Manufacturing costs for May		1,078.00	
		$1,694.00	
Work in process, May 31			80.00
To finished welders			$1,614.00
Finished welders, May 1			637.50
Welders available for sale			$2,251.50
Finished welders, May 31			255.00
Cost of welders sold, May			$1,996.50

ACCOUNTING FOR PROPERTY, PLANT, EQUIPMENT AND OTHER ASSETS

(W.J. Bruns, Jr. / #9-193-046 / 9 p)

Summary

An introduction to depreciation accounting and depreciation methods for capital assets. Also covers gains or losses on asset disposal and accounting for other investments and intangibles.

Outline

The Cost of Fixed Assets

Estimating Depreciation

Gain or Loss on Disposal of Asset

Some Final Comments About Depreciation

Accounting for Land

Accounting for Long-term Investments in Other Organizations

Accounting for Intangible Assets and Goodwill

Learning Objectives

After reading the note and completing the following exercises, managers should be able to:

- Articulate the differences among the three common methods of depreciation.

- Choose an appropriate method for allocating the depreciable cost of a fixed asset in their department.

- Understand how intangible assets are accounted for in financial reports.

Questions and Ideas to Consider

Consider a fixed asset used by your department or unit – a piece of machinery, a computer system, even your office building.

- List all the expenditures that were required to enable you to use that asset. (It's not necessary to give a dollar amount for each expenditure, though an estimate for each would allow you to estimate the total cost of this asset; see Exhibit 1 for an example.)

- How is the depreciable cost of this asset allocated? If you are not sure, which of the three methods discussed on p. 38 would make the most sense? Why?

Accounting for Property, Plant, Equipment and Other Assets

Expenditures for property and capital equipment represent a commitment of some of an organization's resources to investments that are likely to be utilized over several periods. The *matching concept* requires that the cost of such investments be matched with the revenues in the periods in which benefits are obtained by using the capital equipment. For buildings and equipment, the amount of expense matched with revenues is called *depreciation*. If the asset is a natural resource, such as forest land or mineral deposits, similar expenses might be called *depletion*. If the assets are intangible, the original cost is said to be *amortized* over the periods when benefits are obtained, or in some cases, over an arbitrary period.

In practice, accounting for the cost of assets that provide benefits over several periods (also called *fixed assets*) consists of three distinct phases: determining the cost of a fixed asset, amortizing the cost over the useful life of the asset, and removing it from the accounts at the end of the asset's life.

The Cost of Fixed Assets

The cost of the fixed asset and the amount at which it will be initially measured in reports consist of the total amount of expenditures necessary to ready the asset for its intended use. To the price of acquiring legal title to ownership of an asset are added costs of delivery, installation, training of employees, and modification of facilities that are necessary in order to use the asset as planned. (**Exhibit 1** is an illustration of how the cost of a new asset might be measured.)

Estimating Depreciation

At the beginning of the life of an asset, an estimate of the asset's *salvage value* is made. The salvage value is the expected selling price of the asset less any removal costs at the end of its useful life to the organization. The difference between the cost and the salvage value is called the *depreciable cost*, and it is this cost that is to be matched in some way to revenues earned in the accounting periods over which the asset will be used.

Determining depreciation expense using generally accepted accounting principles is not particularly difficult. Having determined depreciable cost, all that remains is to select a method for allocating that cost to periods when the asset will be used to generate revenues. The market prices provided by an asset purchase and an eventual sale provide information about an asset's value at those times. However, in between these points of time, when commonly used depreciation methods are employed, there is no assurance that the asset values are accurately estimated by the unamortized cost reported in the statement of financial position.

In allocating the depreciable cost, any one of several methods is acceptable. Although the methods may appear to be arbitrary, they meet two criteria. The most important criterion requires that the amount of depreciation charged is not subject to manipulation by management in such a way that income for any period can be capriciously distorted. The second criterion is that the amounts charged bear some resemblance to the decline in value of the asset measured on an historical cost basis. There are three methods of depreciation in common use with occasional variations in each: straight-line depreciation, declining balance depreciation, and sum-of-the-years' digits depreciation.

Straight-line Depreciation

Under the straight-line method of depreciation, an equal portion of the depreciable cost is charged according to some measure of the length of an asset's life. The measure may be periods of time, or it may be units of product. Under this method, as under any of the methods of depreciation commonly used, the amount charged to expense is usually accumulated and shown in statements of financial position as a deduction from the historical cost of the asset. This *accumulated depreciation* is called a *contra asset*. It is always associated with the asset to which it is related, and its balance offsets part of the original cost that has already been matched against revenues. **Exhibit 2** shows how depreciation can be estimated using the straight-line method.

Declining Balance Depreciation

In an attempt to reflect the fact that an asset is often most productive in the early years of its use in an organization, accountants often employ methods that charge a larger proportion of the total depreciation expense in the early years of life than in later periods. One common method for accomplishing this is to charge to each period a fixed percentage of the *original cost of the asset less any previously accumulated depreciation* (note the difference from straight-line depreciation in which the depreciation rate is applied to the entire depreciable cost of the asset each period). Commonly, this percentage will be 150% or 200% of the depreciation rate used under the straight-line method. Because the declining balance method will never completely amortize the original cost of an asset, it is customary not to deduct salvage value of the asset from the original cost prior to applying the depreciation percentage. **Exhibit 3** shows how depreciation can be estimated using the declining balance method.

Sum-of-Years' Digits Method

A third depreciation method commonly used in financial reporting in the United States is the sum-of-the-years' digits method. Under this method, depreciation is related to time in annual periods. The numbers used to identify each year of life, from 1 to n, are summed. The depreciation expense for each year is estimated by taking in inverse order the number of the period as the numerator of a fraction having as its denominator the sum-of-the-years of the asset's life. This fraction is multiplied times the depreciable cost, based on cost-less-salvage value, to estimate the year's depreciation expense. One should not waste any time searching for the logic of this method, for there is none. However, it does satisfy the criteria for an acceptable depreciation amount. **Exhibit 4** shows how depreciation can be estimated using the sum-of-the-years' digits method.

Gain or Loss on Disposal of Asset

A decision to sell or otherwise dispose of a fixed asset may come any time after it is acquired. In some cases, assets thought to be useful to the firm will prove not to be so useful. It may be that they are more valuable to the organization when sold for cash. For this reason, assets are sometimes sold before the end of their original expected useful life, so that the resources committed to them can be redeployed more effectively.

In other situations, assets may be held over a longer period of time than expected and employed in their intended uses very profitably. At some point, however, the cost of maintenance and repair necessary to maintain a favorable stream of income for the organization becomes prohibitive, and the asset must be sold or scrapped. In other cases, technological developments will cause an asset to become obsolete. Assets can also be sold or exchanged for another asset. Occasionally, however, an organization may have to pay to have a useless asset destroyed or hauled away.

When an asset is sold or otherwise disposed of, it is usually necessary to account for the fact that earlier estimates about the salvage value or life of the asset were not correct. Differences between the *book value* and the amount actually obtained upon disposal are shown either as a gain or loss in the period in which the asset disposal takes place. Although gains and losses resulting from the disposal of assets represent miscalculations made in other periods, it is usually not considered necessary to adjust estimates of income in those earlier periods except in the most extreme cases.

Typically, the used asset is sold, and the items relating to the asset disappear from the accounts of the firm. We use the difference between the book value of the assets and the amount of cash or other resources received to determine whether or not the gain or loss on disposal of the asset should be recognized. In either case, the cash received from the sale is not included in revenue, and the amount of gain or loss is usually reported separately in the income statement as gain or loss on sale of assets.

Some Final Comments About Depreciation

This note has introduced in a cursory way three methods of allocating as expense all or part of the original cost of an asset over the life of that asset. Other methods have been proposed, and some are employed by business organizations. The importance of the depreciation estimate lies in its relationship to the proper determination of income. While the criterion of accurate estimation of periodic income should dictate the choice of depreciation method, in practice other criteria often dominate: simplicity of application, tax and other legal requirements, or the desire on the part of management to show earnings more favorable or less favorable than those that would be shown if another method were used. Estimates of depreciation expense, therefore, must be used and interpreted with great care.

One other aspect of depreciation accounting deserves mention. We have dealt with the depreciation of individual assets because this was the easiest way to illustrate different methods of depreciation. In practice, however, a large firm may have many assets of a certain type—for example, personal computers. The problems of accounting for acquisition, depreciation, and disposal of these types of assets may not be too different from those encountered when accounting for inventory. Sometimes, when there are large numbers of similar items, rather than keep track of each asset, accountants find it more feasible to depreciate them as a group. A full discussion of methods of *group depreciation* or *composite depreciation* is unnecessary, but you should be aware of the fact that such groupings are frequently used to simplify the recording and reporting tasks.

Accounting for Land

Like other fixed assets, land is recorded in the accounting records at the cost needed to upgrade it to the condition necessary for its intended use. Purchase price, fees or taxes incurred in the purchase, the cost of clearing or grading land, or the cost of developing drainage would all be included in the amount of cost for purchase of a tract of land. In contrast to other fixed assets, land is not depreciated and is held at original cost until such time as it is sold, traded, or abandoned.

Accounting for Long-term Investments in Other Organizations

Organizations often find it in their interest to acquire an investment in companies that they regard as subsidiaries. These investments in subsidiaries are considered long term. If the investment in a subsidiary is 20% or less of the total ownership of the subsidiary, the investment is usually accounted for using a *cost method*. The investment is carried at its original cost in the owning company's accounts, and any dividends are reported as current income.

If the investment in the affiliated company is greater than 20% but less than 50%, the parent company will usually account for the investment using a method known as the *equity method*. In this method, a share of the subsidiary's earnings proportional to the share of company ownership is added to the investment in the company accounts, whether the earnings have been distributed as dividends or not. If dividends are paid by the subsidiary, they reduce the equity investment shown in the parent company's account.

When ownership in a subsidiary exceeds 50% of the total ownership, consolidation of the accounts of both parent and subsidiary on a line-by-line basis is normally required. In these cases, other owners' interest may appear as a liability under the title *minority interest in subsidiaries*.

Accounting for Intangible Assets and Goodwill

In spite of their desire to produce the most useful information and reports, accountants frequently ignore many intangibles in statements of financial position. Unless intangibles have been purchased, it is difficult to estimate their value with any precision. Instead, expenditures for the purposes of developing trademarks or advertising programs which create customer loyalty, or research and development expenditures are expensed in the periods they are incurred. Current income is reduced during the period in which the expenditures are made, and no recognition is given to future benefits that may accrue from these expenditures.

One common intangible asset frequently found in financial reports is *goodwill*. When one company purchases another, paying more than fair value of the net assets of the acquired company, the difference is called goodwill and may be shown as an asset on the balance sheet of the purchasing firm. The amount of goodwill should be expensed against revenue in future periods just as we match the cost of capital assets against the periods when benefits accrue. In the United States, goodwill must be amortized over a period not to exceed 40 years. When goodwill is deemed not to be of any further consequence, it can be written off against the owners' equity of the acquiring organization. In some countries, it is common to make this write-off at the date goodwill is acquired rather than to confuse the reported income in future periods with an expense that represents nothing more than an arbitrary allocation.

Plant assets, intangible assets, and other assets reported by the Gillette Company and Subsidiary Companies in its consolidated balance sheet for 1995 are shown in **Exhibit 5**, along with the associated footnotes. In particular, the notes to financial statements illustrate several of the ideas and financial reporting concepts that have been discussed in this note.

Exhibit 1   Measuring the Cost of a New Asset

Western Metallurgical purchased a new laboratory furnace on January 1, 1992. The price of the new furnace was $13,000, but the manufacturer agreed to allow a trade-in of $3,000 for an old furnace and a $500 discount because Western agreed to pay $9,500 cash for the balance. To the $12,500 given in exchange for the new furnace, the following items were added to the cost of the new asset: $500 for freight charges for delivery, $2,000 paid to an electrician and engineer for installation, and $1,000 paid to reimburse two key employees for expenses incurred while visiting the manufacturer's plant in another city to receive instructions on operating the new equipment. The cost of the asset, and hence a measure of its value on the first day it was ready for operation, was estimated to be $16,000, as shown below.

Cost of New Laboratory Furnace—January 1, 1992		
Cash paid for new furnace:		
Purchase price	$13,000	
Less: Trade-in allowance	3,000	
Less: Discount for cash	500	
	$ 9,500	
Value of old furnace		3,000
Total assets paid		$12,500
Freight charges for delivery		500
Installation costs		2,000
Training costs for employees		1,000
Total cost		$16,000

Exhibit 2   Estimating Straight-line Depreciation

Following the purchase of the new furnace, the management of Western Metallurgical turned to the problem of selecting a method of depreciation. It estimated that the furnace would have a salvage value of $6,000 at the end of its useful life of five years. Thus, the depreciable cost was estimated to be $10,000.

The accountant suggested that the $10,000 depreciable cost could be allocated on a straight-line basis at a rate of $2,000 per year over the five years the furnace would be used. As an alternative, he suggested that the firm might estimate the total number of pounds of metal that would be melted in the furnace over the five-year period and then charge depreciation expense in relation to the amount of metal melted as a proportion of the expected total. Management expected that it would melt about 250,000 pounds of metal in the next five years; therefore in each year, depreciation expense would be calculated by taking the number of pounds of metal melted and multiplying it by $.04. The depreciation expense that might be shown if the straight-line method were adopted is shown below:

Straight-Line Depreciation Schedule for Laboratory Furnace

Depreciable cost:	
Price of furnace	$13,000
Less: Discount	500
	$12,500
Freight charge	500
Installation	2,000
Training expenses	1,000
Total cost	$16,000
Less: Salvage value	6,000
Depreciable cost	$10,000

Estimated life: 5 years

Expected metal melt: 250,000 pounds

Schedule of depreciation expense:

Year	Expected Melt (in pounds)	Time Base	Use Base
1	40,000	$ 2,000	$ 1,600
2	45,000	2,000	1,800
3	50,000	2,000	2,000
4	55,000	2,000	2,200
5	60,000	2,000	2,400
Total	250,000	$10,000	$10,000

Exhibit 3   Estimating Declining Balance Depreciation

Depreciable cost: $16,000

Estimated life: 5 years

Schedule of depreciation expense:

Year	Book Value at Beginning of Year	Depreciation Expense (40% of book value)	Book Value at End of Year
1	$16,000	$ 6,400	$9,600
2	9,600	3,840	5,760
3	5,760	2,304	3,456
4	3,456	1,382	2,074
5	2,074	829	1,245
Total		$14,755	

Management was disturbed by the fact that the use of this method would depreciate the asset by such an amount that the reported value after the second year would be less than the expected salvage value and that it would apparently show a large gain when the asset was sold at the end of its useful life. Its accountant explained that it would be possible to find a percentage rate that would exactly amortize the $10,000 depreciable cost over the five-year period if it preferred to do that rather than use an arbitrary 200% of the straight-line depreciation rate.

Exhibit 4   Estimating Sum-of-Years Digits Depreciation

Sum-of-Years' Digits Depreciation Schedule for Laboratory Furnace

      Depreciable cost: $10,000
      Estimated life: 5 years
      Sum of digits: $1 + 2 + 3 + 4 + 5 = 15$[a]
      Schedule of depreciation expense:

Year	Depreciation Factor	Depreciation Expense
1	5/15	$ 3,333
2	4/15	2,667
3	3/15	2,000
4	2/15	1,333
5	1/15	667
		$10,000

[a] The sum-of-years' digits can be calculated using

$$SYD = \frac{n(n+1)}{2}$$

here SYD = sum-of-years, and n = number of years of life.

Exhibit 5   Noncurrent Assets, The Gillette Company and Subsidiary Companies (Excerpt from Consolidated Balance Sheets) ($ million)

	December 31, 1995	December 31, 1994
Property, plant and equipment, at cost less accumulated depreciation	$1,636.9	$1,411.0
Intangible assets, less accumulated amortization	1,221.4	887.4
Other assets	377.5	314.6

Notes to Consolidated Financial Statements

Property, Plant and Equipment

Land	$ 37.4	$ 36.9
Buildings	509.9	465.8
Machinery and equipment	2,714.2	2,399.5
	3,261.5	2,902.2
Less accumulated depreciation	1,624.6	1,491.2
	$1,636.9	$1,411.0

Intangible Assets

Goodwill ($43.8 million not subject to amortization)	$1,229.4	$ 905.0
Other intangible assets	187.4	148.1
	1,416.8	1,053.1
Less accumulated amortization	195.4	165.7
	$1,221,4	$887.4

Depreciation

Depreciation is computed primarily on a straight-line basis over the estimated useful lives of assets.

Intangible Assets

Intangible assets principally consist of goodwill, which is amortized on the straight-line method, generally over a period of 40 years. Other intangible assets are amortized on the straight-line method over a period of from 13 to 40 years. The carrying amounts of intangible assets are assessed for impairment when operating profit from the applicable related business indicates that the carrying amount of the assets may not be recoverable.

A NOTE ON LIABILITIES AND TIME

(W.J. Bruns, Jr. / #9-193-051 / 14 p)

Summary

An introduction to accounting for liabilities. Both current liabilities and long-term debts are described, and illustrations of bond interest calculations and financial reporting formats are included.

Outline

Current Liabilities

Long-term Debt

> Bonds
> Long-term Leases

Conditional Liabilities

> Product Guarantees
> Postretirement Benefits
> Deferred Taxes

Learning Objectives

After reading the note and completing the following exercises, managers should be able to:

- Become familiar with the basic categories of liabilities on their firm's balance sheet.

- Analyze the liability created by a simple bond issue.

- Understand why conditional liabilities, such as product guarantees, pose special accounting challenges.

Questions and Ideas to Consider

1. Review the liabilities section of your firm's balance sheet. What are your company's primary liabilities? Why do you think this is so?

2. How would you use the concept of conditional liabilities to explain to your colleagues how product or service quality can affect your company's profitability?

A Note on Liabilities and Time

When an organization makes a commitment to an outside party to pay resources at some time in the future, the commitment is a *liability*. If the payment is due within one "operating cycle" (often assumed to be one year) of the organization's activities, the commitment will usually be classified as a *current liability*. *Noncurrent liabilities* are those that will be paid in a subsequent operating cycle or at a time beyond one year. The distinction between short-term liabilities and long-term liabilities is rarely precise. Likewise, the exact time period is rarely critical. Nevertheless, the distinction often determines how an accountant will measure the future burden of the liability, and how it will be reported in financial reports.

Current Liabilities

Short-term or current liabilities of an individual or organization are created by exchanges or events that may involve a variety of sources. For example, accounts payable may be due to many different creditors. Current liabilities are usually labeled according to the party or class of creditor to which payments will be made. Classifications may be broad or narrow, depending upon the amount of detail that managers and their accountants wish to show in financial reports.

Exhibit 1 shows the liabilities reported for the Gillette Company and Subsidiary Companies the end of 1995 and 1994. Additional detail on the amount of liabilities and debt is contained in the notes to financial statements, which are also shown in **Exhibit 1**. Gillette reports four classifications of current liabilities but groups all other liabilities into three classifications.

Many current liabilities arise from transactions involving employees and suppliers. These *accounts payable* report amounts owed to suppliers who have provided materials or services, but who have not yet been paid. This use of credit not only provides resources to the organization incurring a liability but also facilitates activity in that it is not necessary to pause and make payments continuously as transactions take place or services are rendered. Most organizations normally have a significant number of accounts payable. Gillette labels this item *Accounts Payable and Accrued Liabilities*. These include amounts payable to suppliers for purchased goods and services, to employees for wages and salaries that were unpaid at the balance-sheet date, to government agencies as a result of payroll or property taxes, and so forth. If Gillette had wanted to show greater detail, it could have shown other categories in separate classifications.

Professor William J. Bruns prepared this note as the basis for class discussion.

Current liabilities are usually measured using the amount of cash or other assets that would currently satisfy the obligation if it were paid. If interest is associated with a liability, the amount of interest expense already incurred will be added to the original liability incurred. Measuring current liabilities is usually fairly straightforward, and understanding the future burden that they will place on the organization is usually simple, provided sufficient detail has been included in the statement of financial position.

Two kinds of liabilities, *unearned revenue* and *deferred credits*, are often found among current liabilities and deserve special mention. Each shows the obligation of the organization to customers or clients. In many types of businesses, customers pay in advance for services, and in return, the organization promises to provide future services or products. Magazine subscriptions are typically sold on this basis, as are tickets for artistic or athletic events and airline transportation. The amount of resources received in advance for services that have not as yet been provided is clearly a liability. The organization promises to provide a good or service in the future to the same degree of certainty as if it had promised to provide payment in the future. The fact that the obligation will not be settled by payment of cash or assets does not mean a liability does not exist.

These situations result in *unearned revenue*, which is included in current liabilities if the product or service is to be delivered within the next operating cycle. Then, when the product or service is delivered, the revenue previously unearned becomes revenue of that operating period. The expenses to provide the product or service are matched with the revenue recognized in measuring and reporting the income at the time the product or service is delivered.

Deposits received from customers can also create liabilities. Deposits are frequently called *deferred credits*. If the deposit is an advance payment for a product or service, the deposit will be added to other revenues obtained when the product or service is delivered and will be removed from the liability account at that time. Other types of deferred credits might include deposits on shipping containers or other items of value provided by the seller to a customer. The deposit serves as security, and when the container or other items are returned, the refund of the deposit reduces cash and eliminates the liability.

Finally, as time passes, liabilities once classified as long-term come within the reach of the next operating period when they will be satisfied. That portion to be paid in the subsequent operating period is transferred from long-term liability categories to current liabilities, where it may be identified as the *current portion of long-term debt*. Amounts that will not be paid in the next period will continue to be shown as long-term debts.

Long-term Debt

Agreements to pay at some future point of time or at intervals of time in the future represent an important source of resources to many organizations. Such agreements frequently take the form of loan contracts between the organization as a borrower and another individual or entity. They may take the form of debt security, such as debenture bonds, which lenders are free to trade among themselves and which are frequently traded in the securities markets. Loans can take other forms as well and may be known as mortgages, trust notes, or any of a number of other possible types of debt instruments. The characteristics that set these apart from other liabilities are their contractual nature and the extended period over which interest is to be accrued or payments are to be made.

Perhaps the simplest type of long-term debt is a contractual agreement to pay some specified amount at some time in the future. Consider the firm that has agreed to pay $1,000 in cash five years from today to another party.

At first glance, the $1,000 commitment might seem to have a value equal to cash or other resources the organization will have to give up when the debt falls due. Thus, we might simply say the liability has a value of $1,000. On the other hand, if we consider the investment decision of the person with whom we have made this agreement, the creditor, we would surely recognize that the value is less than the $1,000 amount stated in the liability agreement.

Suppose we were to go to the creditor and ask how much we would have to pay today to be released from our future obligation. Alternatively, we might go to a third party and ask it how much we would have to pay it to assume our promise to pay in the future.

Providing the creditor has alternative uses for the resources that we would offer today to cancel our future obligation, we should be able to settle for less than $1,000. If the market rate of interest is 10%, then we might expect that the creditor would accept the present value of $1,000 five years from now, or $620.92 today, and release us from our future commitment.[1] That is the amount that a person would have to invest today to have $1,000 five years hence if the available interest rate is 10%. Actually, we might have to pay slightly more than $620.92 to compensate the creditor for the inconvenience of locating another investment. The nature of the liability compels us to measure its value in terms of what we would have to pay to satisfy the creditor.

When an organization incurs a liability such as a promise of $1,000 to be paid at the end of five years, the proper measurement of the claim is never the amount promised in the future. Instead, it would be the present value considering alternative uses (for five years) of the resources that can be made by any other parties to the contract. Even if the creditor should reject the offer to settle a future commitment at a level reflecting the market rate of interest, there is no reason for concern. The entity committed to a future payment can invest resources at the market rate of interest and thus accumulate the amount necessary to satisfy its obligation when it finally falls due. **Exhibit 2** illustrates how the present burden of a liability can be estimated and related to the amount that will have to be paid when the settlement date of the obligation finally occurs.

Discounting future expenditures to their present value rather than observing only their contractual amount is important for valuing long-term liabilities. Although the same arguments could be applied to current liabilities, the fact that these liabilities will be settled soon usually leads accountants to treat current liabilities as if the difference between the present value of the amount to be paid and the contractual amount is immaterial.

Bonds

The amounts that business firms and other organizations wish to borrow are sometimes quite large—larger than any single lender may be willing or able to provide. For this reason, securities are created. One general category of borrowing instruments is that of bond indentures. The terms of a loan are specified in a master contract between the entity, which is the borrower, and the bondholders, who are the lenders. Each bondholder receives a certificate showing the total indebtedness represented by the certificate and the terms of his or her contract with the firm.

All bond agreements have three basic features:

1.   The *term* of the loan is specified.

2.   A *face amount* of the loan is specified.

---

[1]The present value of $1,000 five years from now can be calculated by the formula:
  Present Value = $1,000 ÷ $(1 + .10)^5$.

3.   The *repayment schedule* is shown either in detailed amounts or as a percentage rate of interest to be paid at intervals based upon the face amount of the bond.

Other terms such as the privilege of conversion to other forms of securities may also be included in some bonds, but for simplicity we will ignore those complications here.

Bonds are typically issued in multiples of $1,000, so let us assume that an organization is offering to sell a bond with a term of 10 years, a face amount of $1,000, and annual payments based on an interest rate of 8%. Now what do these contractual terms mean?

The face amount of the bond determines the amount that the issuers will pay the holder at the end of the life of the bond. In this example, at the end of 10 years, the issuer of the bond will pay to whomever presents it, $1,000. The "nominal" interest rate, 8%, determines the amount of annual payments that will be made in addition to the terminal payment at the end of the bond term. Since that rate in our example is 8%, the annual payments on the $1,000 bond will be $80. For this reason, when the borrower firm offers this bond for sale, it is asking, "How much will you lend me for promises to pay $80 at the end of each year for 10 years and, in addition, for the promise that I will pay $1,000 at the end of 10 years?"[2]

The amount that a lender will be willing to offer for a bond is dependent upon the desired rate of interest, or *yield*, that the lender wishes to earn on the amount about to be invested. **Exhibit 3** illustrates the procedure that three investors might use to decide what to bid on a bond offering, assuming that each is willing to earn a different rate of interest on the investment. The lender willing to bid the highest amount determines the *prevailing market interest rate* for the bonds offered.

The difference between the face amount of the bond and the amount received by the borrower when the bond is initially issued is referred to as discount or premium. If the amount received is *larger* than the face amount, the difference is called *premium*. If it is *smaller*, the difference is called *discount*. Premium or discount results whenever the nominal interest rate, that stated on the face of a bond, is different from the current market rate of interest demanded by lenders. Only after a bond is issued can the borrower determine the *effective interest rate* on the debt. The effective interest rate is the prevailing interest rate determined by the successful bid for the bonds.

The amount of the liability created by issuing a bond includes the premium (or excludes the discount), which will be amortized by the difference between the *interest expense* each period and the *interest payment* actually made. At any given time, the liability will be the face amount of the bond plus or minus the unamortized premium or discount created when the bond was first sold. From **Exhibit 4**, we can surmise that Investor A, who is willing to invest to earn 6% interest, would at any time be willing to allow Eastern Coast Company to buy back the bond for the amount of liability at the beginning of the year, plus current interest not yet paid, plus perhaps a small premium for inconvenience. Near the end of the tenth year, the amount would be about $1,000 plus current interest earned but not paid.

A similar analysis could be applied to bond discounts, except that the positions would be somewhat different. We can see by referring to **Exhibit 3** that if on the day after Eastern Coast had issued the bond to Investor C for $877, the company wished to cancel the agreement, Investor C probably would have been quite willing to accept $1,000 for it. On the other hand, if we assume that other investments offering a 10% interest rate are available and that Investor C would be able to reinvest at the same rate, it would not be surprising to find that Investor C would be willing to cancel

---

[2]By convention, bond interest rates are quoted in annual terms, but one-half of the quoted interest rate is used to determine the amount of *semiannual* interest payments. However, for this illustration annual payments are assumed in order to simplify **Exhibits 3** and **4**.

the future obligations in return for a payment for something near $877.07 plus any current interest already earned but not yet paid.

In accounting for bonds, the reduction in liability due to the fact that the periodic payments on bonds issued at a premium exceed the effective interest is referred to as the *amortization of bond premium*. If bonds are issued at discount, the periodic payments will be less than the effective interest, and the liability will grow because of *amortization of bond discount*. When bonds are issued for exactly the face amount, there is no premium or discount to amortize, and since the effective rate of interest is equal to the stated rate, interest each period will be equal to the periodic payments. You should note that as the liability differs in each succeeding year due to amortization of premium or discount, so will the amount of interest expense change, even though the annual payment set by the contract will remain the same.

Exhibit 5 provides another illustration, somewhat more extensive than **Exhibits 3** and **4**, of a proposed bond issue.

If all bonds were as simple as those we have used here to illustrate the problems of accounting for long-term debt, observing, measuring, and reporting on liabilities of this type would be much easier than they frequently are in practice. As the number of conditions attached to a bond increases or the options open to either the bondholder (for example, the right to turn in the bond in return for ownership shares) or the borrower (for example, the right to pay off the bond at a specified sum at any point of time during its life) multiply, the more difficult become the problems of accounting for bonds.

Long-term Leases

Many organizations secure the future benefits of land, buildings, and equipment through lease agreements rather than through purchase. A lease agreement conveys to the organization the right to use a resource in return for a promise to pay a specified amount at some future time or at many times in the future. The owner of property or equipment who enters into such an agreement is called a *lessor*; the entity that secures the rights to use the resources in return for a promise to pay is called the *lessee*.

The terms of lease agreements vary widely. Some are for long periods, others are for short. Some demand that the lessee pay all expenses in maintaining and using the property, while others confer on the lessee the rights of use but leave the burdens of maintenance and replacement on the lessor.

Organizations that lease assets rather than purchase them may do so for a number of reasons. In many cases, leasing provides a type of financing. The products and benefits of using resources can be obtained through leasing without paying for them until receipts can be obtained from customers. This frees the firm from the necessity of other forms of borrowing and preserves liquid assets. In some instances, lease agreements are only veiled purchase agreements. This is particularly true when payments are to be made over a period of time, after which legal title to the leased property is transferred to the lessee.

Since a lease agreement requires the outflow of cash or other resources in the future, it has the essential characteristics of a liability. In many cases, this liability resembles long-term bonds, and the problem of accounting for the liability is quite similar to that for bonds. Because of their kinship to long-term liabilities, we might expect to find lease agreements included with long-term debts when reports on liabilities or the value of the firm are prepared. However, in practice, at least in public reports, long-term leases and their related obligations are often only reported in footnotes. Only when lease agreements are essentially agreements to purchase and simply provide a means for the buyer to delay payment for the assets do generally accepted accounting principles call for full disclosure of the liability inherent in the lease agreement.

Conditional Liabilities

An important class of liabilities to many business organizations is one in which the promises to pay are contingent upon the occurrence of other events. Product guarantees and pension payments are two important types of conditional liabilities. When an entity promises to expend resources if certain events occur, a *conditional liability* has been created.

The observation and measurement problems associated with conditional liabilities are somewhat more difficult than those for contractual liabilities, but not impossibly so. The accountant must consider what the probable payments may be and then calculate the present value of the expected future payments.

Product Guarantees

Often a business firm, in order to promote a product, will promise to refund the purchase price if the product fails to satisfy the customer. Alternatively, a replacement unit or cash refund based on use may be offered. Products returned under the guarantee rarely have any resale value. They have been used, and therefore they are often either given away or destroyed. The amount of liability created by such an agreement depends upon the frequency with which customers return the product and on the terms of the guarantee. The frequency will, in turn, be dependent upon factors, many of which are not easily measurable even when they are observed by the accountant. Product quality, product price, consumer expectations, and other factors all enter into the individual consumer's decision process in considering whether to return a product for refund. Despite the difficulty of projecting possible costs under product guarantees, it can be important in some circumstances. Thus, the accountant must employ as much ingenuity as possible in attempting to observe, measure, and report them.

Postretirement Benefits

Frequently, in order to increase the attractiveness of employment or to reward faithful service, an entity enters into an agreement with its employees to provide them with a pension or other benefits on their retirement. A pension is a promise to pay a specified amount periodically for a specified period of time. Typically, a pension agreement guarantees that a certain amount will be paid each month to an employee after he or she retires. The conditional nature of such a liability makes the measurement difficult, for many factors can change during the years that intervene before an employee's retirement date arrives and the payments begin. Furthermore, the period of time over which the payments must be made depends upon whether employees die before retirement, soon after, or live for many years.

A postretirement agreement consists in most cases of a fairly long list of promises with stipulations. Typically, it provides that a specified amount will be paid periodically or as a lump sum, provided that the employee has met certain conditions: that he or she has continued in the employment of the entity until his or her retirement; that he or she has served some minimum of time prior to retirement; and that he or she has contributed some proportion of the amount necessary to make payments. The amounts of payments may vary depending upon the salary earned for all employees.

In practice, liabilities for pensions are sometimes eliminated by paying premiums to insurance or other fiduciary or trust agencies which then assume the liability. Since the liability is transferred to another organization, the liability is no longer a liability of the organization that created it.

As in the case of any other long-term liability, the amount of pension liability can be affected by a change in the agreement, by a change in the work force resulting in older or younger employees, or by a change in the rate at which future payments are discounted. Environmental events can have an important impact on the amount of the liability and should be reflected in accounting for pension liabilities.

Deferred Taxes

When the amount of income taxes paid differs from the tax expense that should be reported in financial reports, the difference is recorded and reported as *deferred taxes*. Measuring and reporting deferred taxes create some of the most complicated reporting problems accountants face because of the complexity of income tax regulations and the conditional nature of income taxes not yet due.

Summary

Liabilities are commitments to transfer resources to another person or organization at some time in the future. Current liabilities are usually measured and reported at the amount that will be paid to satisfy the claims of creditors. Long-term liabilities are usually reported at the present value of the amounts of claim or estimates of what will eventually be paid.

On a balance sheet, liabilities show the sources other than owners' contributions and retained earnings of the resources (assets) of the organization. Just as assets must be managed, liabilities need attention to make the best use of this important source of resources while preserving the credit worthiness of the organization.

Exhibit 1   The Gillette Company and Subsidiary Companies—Liabilities (Excerpt from Consolidated Balance Sheets) ($ millions)

	December 31,	
	1995	**1994**
Liabilities and Stockholders' Equity		
Current Liabilities		
Loans payable	$ 576.2	$ 344.4
Current portion of long-term debt	26.5	28.1
Accounts payable and accrued liabilities	1,273.3	1,178.2
Income taxes	248.0	185.5
Total current liabilities	$2,124.0	$1,736.2
Long-term Debt	$ 691.1	$ 715.1
Deferred Income Taxes	72.7	53.1
Other Long-term Liabilities	919.2	774.3
Minority Interest	20.0	17.4

Notes to Consolidated Financial Statements

ACCOUNTS PAYABLE AND ACCRUED LIABILITIES

(Millions of dollars)	December 31,	
	1995	**1994**
Accounts payable	$ 400.3	$ 334.6
Advertising and sales promotion	227.5	218.0
Payroll and payroll taxes	221.3	197.8
Other taxes	71.1	45.5
Interest payable	8.8	12.2
Dividends payable on common stock	66.7	55.4
Realignment expense	30.2	107.3
Miscellaneous	247.4	207.4
	$1,273.3	$1,178.2

INCOME TAXES

Beginning in 1993, deferred taxes are provided for using the asset and liability method for temporary differences between financial and tax reporting.

DEBT

Loans payable at December 31, 1995 and 1994, included $223 million and $142 million, respectively, of commercial paper. The company's commercial paper program is supported by its revolving credit facilities.

Long-term debt is summarized as follows.

(Millions of dollars)	December 31,	
	1995	**1994**
Commercial paper	$150.0	$150.0
5.75% Notes due 2005	200.0	200.0
6.25% Notes due 2003	150.0	150.0
4.75% Notes due 1996	150.0	150.0
8.03% Guaranteed ESOP notes due through 2000	41.2	51.5
Other, primarily foreign currency borrowings	26.4	41.7
Total long-term debt	$717.6	$743.2
Less current portion	26.5	28.1
Long-term portion	$691.1	$715.1

OTHER LONG-TERM LIABILITIES

Pensions	$449.6	$368.4
Postretirement medical	209.1	193.1
Incentive plans	131.6	116.6
Realignment expense	(11.0)	15.0
Miscellaneous	139.9	81.2
	$919.2	$744.3

Exhibit 1 (continued)

At December 31, 1995 and 1994, the company had swap agreements that converted $500 million in U.S. dollar-denominated long-term fixed rate debt securities into multicurrency principal and floating interest rate obligations over the term of the respective issues. As of December 31, 1995, the $150 million notes due 1996 were swapped into floating interest rate U.S. dollar obligations, the $150 million notes due 2003 and the $200 million notes due 2005 were swapped to Deutschmark principal and floating interest rate obligations, resulting in an agreement principal amount of $533 million at a weighted average interest rate of 4.7%. At December 31, 1994, the aggregate principal amounted to $500 million, with a weighted average interest rate of 5.6%

In addition, at December 31, 1995, the company had a forward exchange contract, maturing in 1996, that established a $42 million Yen principal, .5% interest obligation with respect to $43 million of U.S. dollar commercial paper debt included in Long-Term Debt. At December 31, 1994, the Company had forward exchange contracts that established Deutschmark and Yen principal and interest obligations with respect to $119 million of U.S. dollar commercial paper debt included in Long-Term Debt, with a weighted average interest rate of 3.7%.

Exchange rate movements give rise to changes in the values of these agreements that offset changes in the values of the underlying exposure. Amounts associated with these agreements were liabilities of $32.6 million at December 31, 1995, and were nil at December 31, 1994.

The weighted average interest rate on Loans payable was 5.8% at December 31, 1995, and 6.5% at December 31, 1994. The weighted average interest rate on total long-term debt, including associated swaps and excluding the guaranteed ESOP notes, was 4.7% at December 31, 1995, compared with 5.3% at December 31, 1994.

The company has a $100 million revolving bank credit agreement that expires in June 1996 and a $300million revolving bank credit agreement expiring in June 2000, both of which may be used for general corporate purposes. Under the agreements, the company has the option to borrow at various interest rates, including the prime rate, and is required to pay a weighted average facility fee of 0.65% per annum. At year-end 1995 and 1994, there were no borrowings under these agreements.

Based on the company's intention and ability to maintain its $300 million revolving credit agreement beyond 1996, $150 million of commercial paper borrowings and the $150 million notes due 1996 were classified as long-term debt at December 31, 1995. As of December 31, 1994, $150 million of commercial paper borrowings was so classified.

Aggregate maturities of total long-term debt for the five years subsequent to December 31, 1995, are $176.5 million, $15.1 million, $10.7 million, $8.8 million and $5.1 million, respectively.

Unused lines of credit, including the revolving credit facilities, amounted to $1.02 billion at December 31, 1995.

Exhibit 2   The Value of a Promise to Pay $1,000 at the End of Five Years (rate of interest = 10%)

End of Year	Total Liability, Which Is Equal to the Amount of Creditor's Investment	Interest Accumulated During Year
5	$1,000.00	$90.91
4	909.09	82.64
3	826.45	75.13
2	751.32	68.30
1	683.02	62.10
Now	620.92	

Exhibit 3   Analysis of a Bond by Three Investors

Eastern Coast Company—Analysis of Value of 10-Year, 8%, $1,000 Bonds to Three Investors Who Seek 6%, 8%, and 10% Return, Respectively

---

Investor A demands 6%.
Investor B demands 8%.
Investor C demands 10%.

Bond contract ("indenture") promises:
a) Ten payments of $80 at end of each of 10 years.
b) One payment of $1,000 at end of 10 years.

Present Value of $1.00	At 6% Interest	At 8% Interest	At 10% Interest
Received annually for 10 years	7.3601	6.7101	6.1446
Received at end of 10 years	.5584	.4632	.3855

Value to Investors at Issue Date

A		B		C	
7.3601 X $ 80 =	$ 588.81	6.701 X $ 80 =	$ 536.80	6.1446 X $ 80 =	$491.57
.5584 X 1,000 =	558.40	.4632 X 1,000 =	463.20	.3855 X 1,000 =	385.50
Total	$1,147.21[a]	Total	$1,000.00	Total	$877.07
A will pay a premium of $147.21 over the face amount of the bond.		B will pay the face amount of $1,000.		C demands a discount of $122.93 off the face amount of the bond.	

---

[a]The value of the liability and hence the amount that the business firm issuing this bond will receive are dependent on the rate of return that the investors wish to earn on their investment. Because Investor A demands only 6% on his or her investment, he or she is willing to lend more, given the fixed terms of the contract. The entity issuing these bonds would be foolish not to accept his or her high bid of $1,147.21 for the bond.

Exhibit 4   A Investment in a Bond from the Investor's Point of View

Assume that the Eastern Coast Company issued the bond described in **Exhibit 3** to Investor A and received $1,147.21 from him or her. Investor A has accepted a yield rate of interest of 6%, which is the rate of interest Eastern Coast now will pay on the *actual* amount borrowed. Its original promises remain constant, however; it will make 10 payments of $80 at the end of each year for 10 years and 1 payment of $1,000 at the end of 10 years.

If the original liability of Eastern Coast is assumed to be equal to the amount received, the table below shows how that liability increases during each year because of the interest owed to Investor A, then falls as each $80 payment is made until at the end of 10 years it is exactly equal to the $1,000 terminal payment originally promised.

Year	Liability at Beginning of Year	Interest at 6% = Yield Rate	Liability at End of Year Before Payment	Payment	Liability at End of Year
1	$1,147.21	$ 68.83[a]	$1,216.04	$ 80.00	$1,136.04
2	1,136.04	68.16	1,204.20	80.00	1,124.20
3	1,124.20	67.45	1,191.65	80.00	1,111.65
4	1,111.65	66.69	1,178.34	80.00	1,098.34
5	1,098.34	65.90	1,164.24	80.00	1,084.24
6	1,084.24	65.05	1,149.29	80.00	1,069.29
7	1,069.29	64.16	1,133.45	80.00	1,053.45
8	1,053.45	63.21	1,116.66	80.00	1,036.66
9	1,036.66	62.20	1,098.86	80.00	1,018.86
10	1,018.86	61.14	1,080.00	80.00	1,000.00
10	-	-	1,000.00	1,000.00	0.00
Totals		$652.79		$1,800.00	

Total borrowed	$1,147.21
Add interest	652.79
Total paid	$1,800.00

[a]We can calculate the interest Investor A expects during the first year by multiplying the amount received by the interest rate used by Investor A (6.0%) originally to value the promised cash payments.

Exhibit 5   Proposed Bond Issue of Indet Corporation

The Indet Corporation is planning to issue bonds with a face value of $1,000,000, bearing a nominal interest rate of 5%, and payable at the end of 20 years. Interest is to be paid semiannually. The treasurer of the corporation has prepared three schedules to show the way in which the liability of the corporation will change over the life of the bonds under varying conditions with respect to yield rates. That is, if the prevailing market interest rate at the date the bonds are issued will be either 4%, 5%, or 6% interest return, the measurement of the liability will be affected as shown in these schedules (**Exhibits 5a, 5b,** and **5c**).

The schedules of liability prepared by the treasurer show some important features of long-term liabilities with contractual payments that have the same form as bonds. Until the last period, all payments remain the same. When payments are made semiannually, the annual rate of interest must be adjusted to reflect the time period stated for interest. In this case, since payments are to be made semiannually, the interest expense for each period is calculated using half the annual rate. The interest expense is based on the total outstanding liability at the beginning of the period. In cases where premium or discount has been created because the bonds sold at a yield rate different from the stated rate, the difference between the semiannual payment and the interest expense amortizes premium or discount as the case may demand. By the end of the last period of the life of the bonds, the liability is the amount equal to the terminal payment, which includes repayment of principle as well as payment of interest for the last period.

Exhibit 5a   Indet Corporation—Projected Liability at Selected Intervals Due to Sale of $1,000,000, 5%, 20-Year Bonds with Interest Due Semiannually, Sold to Yield 4% to Investors

Interest Period (6 months)	Total Liability at Beginning of Period	Unamortized Premiums	Interest Expense for Period at 4% (2% for 6 months)	Liability at End of Period before Payment	Payment at End of Period	Liability at End of Period after Payment
1	$1,136,787	$136,787	$22,735	$1,159,522	$ 25,000	$1,134,522
2	1,134,522	134,552	22,690	1,157,212	25,000	1,132,212
.	.	.	.	.	.	.
.	.	.	.	.	.	.
20	1,085,080	85,080	21,702	1,106,782	25,000	1,081,872
.	.	.	.	.	.	.
.	.	.	.	.	.	.
40	1,004,902	4,902	20,098	1,025,000	1,025,000	0

Exhibit 5b   Indet Corporation—Projected Liability at Selected Intervals Due to Sale of $1,000,000, 5%, 20-Year Bonds with Interest Due Semiannually, Sold to Yield 5% to Investors

Interest Period (6 months)	Total Liability at Beginning of Period	Unamortized Premiums	Interest Expense for Period at 5% (2-1/2% for 6 months)	Liability at End of Period before Payment	Payment at End of Period	Liability at End of Period after Payment
1	$1,000,000	$0	$25,000	$1,025,000	$ 25,000	$1,000,000
2	1,000,000	0	25,000	1,025,000	25,000	1,000,000
.	.	.	.	.	.	.
20	1,000,000	0	25,000	1,025,000	25,000	1,000,000
.	.	.	.	.	.	.
40	1,000,000	0	25,000	1,025,000	1,025,000	0

Exhibit 5c   Indet Corporation—Projected Liability at Selected Intervals Due to Sale of $1,000,000, 5%, 20-Year Bonds with Interest Due Semiannually, Sold to Yield 6% to Investors

Interest Period (6 months)	Total Liability at Beginning of Period	Unamortized Premiums	Interest Expense for Period at 6% (3% for 6 months)	Liability at End of Period before Payment	Payment at End of Period	Liability at End of Period after Payment
1	$884,470	$115,530	$26,534	$911,004	$25,000	$886,004
2	886,004	113,996	26,580	912,584	25,000	887,584
.	.	.	.	.	.	.
20	922,875	77,125	27,686	950,561	25,000	925,561
.	.	.	.	.	.	.
40	995,146	4,854	29,854	1,025,000	1,025,000	0

LIABILITY REPORTING

(P.M. Healy / #9-101-016 / 5 p)

Summary

Discusses liability recognition, beginning with key criteria for recognizing a liability. Explores liability recognition in straightforward situations and then examines the most difficult reporting issues in recording liabilities, which arise when: 1) uncertainty arises about whether an obligation has been incurred; or 2) measuring the value of the obligation is difficult.

Outline

1. **Uncertainty Over Whether Obligation Incurred**

2. **Measuring Obligations**

Summary

Learning Objectives

After reading the note and completing the following exercises, managers should be able to:

- Grasp the key criteria for recognizing a liability.

- Better understand how their firm reports liabilities that are difficult to measure.

Questions and Ideas to Consider

Review the liabilities section of your firm's balance sheet. How has your firm recorded such liabilities as a pension plan, leases, and warranties? Use the "Liability Reporting" note to guide you in understanding why these items have been reported in this way.

PAUL M. HEALY

Liability Reporting[1]

Liabilities are defined as probable obligations to transfer assets or to provide services to another entity as a result of past transactions.[2] Under accrual accounting, liabilities can arise in three ways. First, a firm can receive cash from a customer but has yet to fulfill its contractual obligations required for recognizing revenue. For example, if a professional football team receives cash from advance ticket sales, it records a deferred revenue liability until it has actually played the games. Second, a firm agrees to make future payments to suppliers, customers, or other stakeholders for goods and services that have been received, for product failures, or for other claims on the firm. Finally, liabilities arise when firms borrow debt capital from banks, financial institutions and the public.

The historical cost concept, discussed for the valuation of assets, is also used to value many liabilities.[3] Thus, financial reports typically do not reflect any change in the value of debt instruments that have fixed interest payments, even though their market values change with fluctuations in interest rates. In the United States firms are currently required to report the market value of debt instruments in their financial statement footnotes. As accountants have become more confident that fair values of liabilities can be estimated reliably, there has even been consideration given to requiring U.S. firms to value all liabilities at fair values.

As shown in **Figure A**, under accrual accounting liabilities are reflected in the financial statements when a firm incurs an obligation to another party for which the amount and timing are measurable with reasonable certainty.

---

[1] For a more comprehensive discussion of this topic, see Chapter 5 of Palepu, Healy, and Bernard, 200, *Business Analysis and Valuation Using Financial Statements*, Second Edition (South-Western, Cincinnati, OH).

[2] Notice that accounting spends considerable effort to define and measure assets and liabilities, but very little effort worrying about equity. Equity is treated as a residual. It is the balance of assets less liabilities. This residual notion is actually quite appropriate since equity can be viewed as a residual claim on the firm.

[3] Exceptions include pension and post-retirement benefit obligations.

Professor Paul M. Healy and Research Associate Preeti Choudhary prepared this note as the basis for class discussion.

Figure A   Criteria for Recording Liabilities

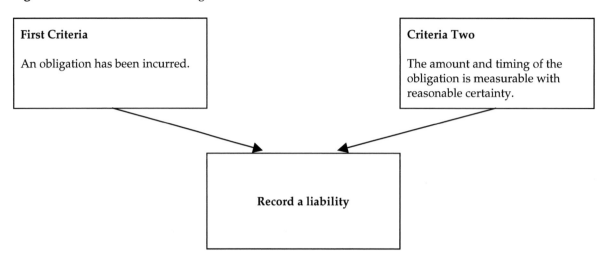

Given these criteria, the most difficult reporting issues in recording liabilities arise when:

- uncertainty arises about whether an obligation has been incurred, or

- measuring the value of the obligation is difficult.

1. Uncertainty Over Whether Obligation Incurred

In some situations assessing whether a firm has actually incurred an obligation is challenging. Examples include assignments of cash flows from receivables to financial institutions and legal actions taken against a company.

Consider a company that assigns to a bank the cash flows from a note receivable. Has the firm effectively sold its receivables? If so, the firm's cash balance would improve and the receivable would be eliminated from its balance sheet. Alternatively, has the firm simply used the receivables as collateral for a bank loan? In this latter case, the transaction still improves the firm's cash position, the receivables continue to be reported as an asset, and a liability is created to reflect the obligation to the bank. The key to distinguishing between these possibilities is whether the company has truly given up control over the receivable cash flows to the bank, or has simply used the receivable as collateral for a bank loan.

Questions over whether a liability has been incurred also arise when a firm is subject to litigation. Does the plaintive company have an obligation for possible losses arising from a law suit or regulatory action? Or is a commitment only incurred when the company loses the case and any damages become known? As discussed in the note on the recognition of expenses, typically, a company is not required to incur a liability when a case is first brought against it. A liability will be recorded only if there is a sufficiently high likelihood of a loss or settlement, and the amount of the loss can be reasonably estimated.

2. *Measuring Obligations*

Many liabilities specify the amount and timing of the obligations precisely. For example, a twenty year $100 million bond issue with an 8% coupon rate payable semi-annually, specifies that the issuer will pay the holders $100 million in twenty years, and will pay out interest of $4 million every six months for the duration of the loan.

However, for some liabilities questions arise about estimating the amount of the obligation. Examples include obligations for lease financing, customer warranties, insurance claim losses, and pension and other post-retirement benefit plans.

Consider first the case of lease financing. As discussed in the note on asset reporting, firms are required to distinguish between operating leases and capital leases. Accounting rules require that capital leases, where control over the leased asset is effectively transferred to the lessee, be recorded as if the company had acquired the leased asset using bank financing. A long-term asset and lease obligation, therefore, appear on the lessee's balance sheet. In contrast, no liability or asset is reported for an operating lease. Leases therefore create two questions for management. First, has a liability been incurred (i.e. is the lease an operating or capital lease)? As discussed in the note on asset reporting, management can influence this outcome since, under current accounting rules, it can often write the lease terms to make the lease satisfy the definition of either type of lease.

A second question for lease reporting is how to value lease obligations for capital leases. The lease contract specifies the lease payments but does not explicitly define the lease obligation or the interest rate. Consistent with the valuation of other obligations, the lease commitment is recorded at the present value of the lease payments computed using a market-based rate of interest at the time when the lease contract is signed. Subsequent lease payments are divided into repayment of the lease obligation and interest expense using the present value method. For example, assume the lease payments are $2m for two years and the market rate of interest on an equivalent loan at the time the lease contract is signed is 10%. When the lease contract is signed, the present value of the lease payments is $3.47m.[4] The loan and subsequent payment have the following financial statement effects:

Cash	+ Other Assets	= Liabilities and Capital	+ Retained Earnings = Beg. RE + NI – Divs)
Sign lease contract			
	Lease asset $3.47m	Lease liability $3.47m	
Make first lease payment			
$(2m)		Lease liability $(1.65m)	Interest expense $(0.35m)
Make second lease payment			
$(2m)		Lease liability $(1.82m)	Interest expense $(0.18m)

---

[4] $3.47 = \dfrac{\$2.0m}{1.1} + \dfrac{\$2.0m}{1.1^2}$

Under the present value method the interest expense each year is the market interest rate (10%) times the lease obligation outstanding at the beginning of the year. For the first year this is 10% * $3.47m = $0.35m. The difference between the total lease payment ($2m) and the interest expense is then considered a repayment of the lease obligation. Since the beginning balance of the obligation diminishes each year with repayments, the interest expense each year will decline. Recall from the Asset Reporting note that the leased asset is amortized using straight-line depreciation.

Commitments to customers for product warranties are also difficult to measure. The revenues associated with the product sale are typically recognized at the time the product is delivered, yet the warranty expenses associated with the sale are unknown at that time. How should these be reported in the financial statements? Should a liability be created when sales are recognized to reflect an estimate of the costs of returns or repairs? Alternatively, should firms wait until returns actually occur before recognizing the financial implications of the warranty commitment? The matching principle of accounting requires that firms match the expected warranty expense with revenues and establish a liability for probable losses that have been incurred at the financial statement date. For example, suppose a firm in its first year of operation offers a one-year warranty on its products. Management estimates that warranty costs on sales for the first year will be $10m, but in the subsequent periods actual warranty costs amount to $12m. The financial statement effects of these events would be as follows:

Cash	+ Other Assets	= Liabilities and Capital	+ Retained Earnings (= Beg. RE + NI – Divs)
Estimate warranty obligation for first-year sales			
		Warranty liability $10m	Warranty expense $(10m)
Subsequent actual customer returns under warranty			
$(12m)		Warranty liability $(12m)	

Note that we actually under-estimated the warranty liability and expense in the first year. This has caused the liability to be -$2m at the end of the warranty period. An additional $2m of warranty expense, therefore, needs to be recorded in the warranty period to make up for the earlier under-estimate.

A similar type of obligation arises for claim losses yet to be paid by insurance companies. Insurance companies typically recognize revenues before the amount and timing of claims for each period has been fully resolved. At the end of the period insurance managers have to estimate the expected costs of unreported claims and reported claims where the claim amount has not yet been settled. Management bases its estimates on reported claims and estimates of costs of settlement, as well as historical data and experience in estimating unreported losses.

A final example of a liability that is difficult to estimate is for defined benefit pension and benefit plans. Many firms make commitments to employees under defined benefit plans for pre-specified pension or retirement benefits at some point in the future. For proper financial reporting, management must estimate the timing and expected future payments to current and past employees for pension benefits, a difficult task requiring actuarial estimates of length of service, time of retirement, length of life, and perhaps future salary increases. The pension obligation is the present value of these expected future benefits. This obligation is offset by the value of any funds that the company has set aside in the pension trust to meet its pension and benefit obligations.

Summary

A liability is an obligation to provide future benefits to another entity as a result of past events, and for which a value can be estimated with reasonable certainty. Liabilities continue to be recorded at their historical cost on the balance sheet. For multi-year commitments, the value of the liability under historical cost is the present value of the expected future commitments, where the discount rate is the rate prevailing when the obligation was created.

Valuation of liabilities can be challenging if uncertainty exists about whether an obligation has been incurred, as is the case for assignments of receivables to banks and litigation. Also, valuation is difficult if the obligation is not specified contractually. In such cases, considerable management judgment is required to value the obligation. Examples include warranty reserves and insurance loss reserves (which require management forecast future warranty and insurance claims), and pension and benefit obligations (where management has to estimate any expected pension payments or benefits owed to past and current employees).

Because the reported liabilities for the firm represent managers' estimates, there is potential concern as to whether investors have complete information on all of the firm's commitments. If managers want to present a balance sheet that shows little debt financing, they may face pressure to understate the firm's liabilities. Investors therefore rely heavily on the auditor, security market regulators and financial analysts to monitor managers' liability reporting decisions. Auditors can have a difficult time discovering unrecorded liabilities. They find it easier to test for over-stated assets, and have to be much more diligent to ferret out the existence of future obligations not yet recorded on the firm's books.

ACCOUNTING FOR INCOME TAXES

(D.F. Hawkins / #9-100-035 / 7 p)

Summary

Discussion and illustration of deferred tax accounting methods, concepts, and practices.

Outline

Tax Expense Components

SFAS 109

> Temporary Differences
> Balance Sheet Approach
> Comprehensive Approach
> Valuation Allowance
> Enacted Change in Tax Laws or Rates
> Tax Allocations
> Exemptions
> Display

Financial Analysis

Learning Objectives

After reading the note and completing the following exercises, managers should be able to:

- Understand how SFAS 109 recognizes and measures deferred tax liabilities and assets.

- Analyze the tax expense note in their firm's financial statement.

Questions and Ideas to Consider

Review the tax expense note from your firm's most recent financial statement, using as a guide the eight points at the end of "Accounting for Income Taxes."

- What does this information reveal about your firm's accounting methods?

- What does this information reveal about your firm's financial health?

- Do you see anything unusual in the note? If so, how could you find out more?

Accounting for Income Taxes

Statement of Financial Accounting Standards No. 109, "Accounting for Income Taxes"(SFAS 109), states that the objectives of income taxes accounting are to recognized 1) the amount of taxes payable or refundable for the current year based on a company's current tax returns and 2) deferred tax liabilities and assets for the future tax consequences of its current and past recognition and measurement differences between its tax returns and its financial statements. These accounting differences arise because the U.S. tax code permits the accounting practices that differ from those used in their financial reports.

Income tax data can be very useful to statement users. They provide an alternative measure of corporate profits that is typically determined by more cash based and conservative accounting practices than those used to determine book income. The detailed notes explaining the elements of the deferred tax assets, and liabilities and the reasons why the company's book tax rate and the statutory rate differ can provide insights into the quality of a company's earnings; reveal possible accounting manipulations; identify the contribution of tax rate management to the levels and change in reporting earnings; facilitate the deaccrual of net income to a cash basis; and help readers estimate the effect of changes in the tax code on a company's earnings and cash flows.

Tax Expense Components

The tax expense (credit) of a corporation consists of two components—current tax expense (credit) and deferred tax expense (credit).

The current tax component is straightforward. Its obligation to make tax payments to or receive tax credits based on the company's tax returns for the period covered by the income statement. For example, if a company's foreign and domestic tax returns show a combined taxable income of $20 million and a tax payment obligation of $8 million, the current portion of the company's tax expense is $8 million. The accounting entry is ($ million):

Dr. Tax expense—current   8
    Cr. Taxes payable   8

Professor David Hawkins prepared this note from published sources. It is a rewritten version of an earlier note.

The deferred tax component is more complicated. The objective in accounting for deferred taxes is to recognize in current financial statements the future tax consequences of past and current events that have been recognized in a company's financial statements or tax returns that result in differences between the tax bases and the financial reporting amounts of a company's assets and liabilities.

To illustrate, assume the ABC Company buys an asset for $100, which it expenses immediately for tax purposes. For financial reporting purposes, it depreciates the asset over a two-year period using the straight-line method (i.e., $50 depreciation per year). The company's taxable income and profit before taxes and charges related to the asset is $200 in both years. The statutory tax rate is 40%.

The asset's tax bases and its net book (financial reporting) value at the end of years one and two are

Asset's Tax Bases and Net Book Vale			
Yearend	Tax Bases	Net Book Value	Difference
1	0*	$50**	$50
2	0	0	0

*(100-100)
** (100-50)

The different year one treatment of the asset's cost for taxable income determination and financial reporting purposes, results in a difference between the asset's tax bases and book value at the end of year one. This difference is temporary. It is eliminated during year two. Deferred tax accounting recognizes the future tax consequences of the temporary difference between the asset's tax bases and book value at the end of year one.

The company's tax return for years one and two is

Year	Taxable Income	Current Tax Obligation
1	$100*	$40**
2	200	80**

*(200-100)
**(taxable income x .4)

If the company only reported a tax expense equal to its current tax obligation and its net income would be

Year	Profit Before Taxes	Current Tax Expense	Net Income
1	$150*	$40**	$110
2	150	80***	70
	$300	$120	$180

*(200-50)
**(100 x .4)
***(200 x .4)

Clearly, if only the current tax obligation was reported as the company's tax expense for year one, year one's net income would be a poor indicator of the potential year two net income.

Deferred tax accounting was adopted to correct such misleading inferences. It recognizing a deferred tax expense in year 1 to reflect the fact that the year one tax treatment of the asset (100 percent charged in year one) has future tax consequences (higher taxable income and tax obligation in year two). The year one deferred tax liability and expense is equal to the tax equivalent of the difference between the asset's tax bases and book value at the end of year one. For example,

Year	Profit Before Taxes	Tax Expense		Net Income	Deferred Tax Liability
		Current	Deferred		
1	$150	$40	$20*	$90	$20
2	150	80	(20)	90	0
	$300	$120	$ 0	$180	$ 0

*(50 x .4)

The deferred tax expense and credit is the difference between the assets' tax and book basis (+50 and –50) times the tax rate.

The deferred tax accounting entries for the two years are:

Year 1: Dr. Deferred tax expense   20
       Cr. Deferred tax liability   20
Year 2: Dr. Deferred tax liability   20
       Cr. Deferred tax expense   20

If the company had reversed the treatment of the asset's cost (i.e., charged 100% of the cost for financial reporting purposes in year one and over two years for tax obligation determination purposes), a deferred tax asset would have been recorded at the end of year one. The accounting entries would be

Year 1: Dr. Deferred tax asset   20
       Cr. Deferred tax credit   20
Year 2: Dr. Deferred tax expense   20
       Cr. Deferred tax asset   20

These entries reflect the following account balances.

Year	Profit Before Taxes	Tax Expense		Net Income	Deferred Tax Asset
		Current	Deferred		
1	$100	$60*	$(20)**	$60	$20
2	200	60	20	120	0
	$300	$120	$ 0	$180	$ 0

*(150 x .4)

**(50 x .4)

SFAS 109

SFAS 109 adopts the asset-liability approach to the recognition and measurement of a company's deferred tax liabilities and assets. The following basic principles are used to account for income taxes.

1. A current tax liability or asset is recognized for the estimated taxes payable or refundable on the current year tax returns.

2. A deferred tax liability or asset is recognized for the estimated future tax effects attributable to temporary differences and carryforwards

3. The measurement of current and deferred tax liabilities and assets is based on provisions of the enacted tax law; the effects of future changes in tax laws or rates are not anticipated.

4. The measurement of deferred tax assets is reduced, if necessary, by the amount of any tax benefits that, based on available evidence, are not expected to be realized.

Temporary Differences

There are four types of temporary differences. The transaction giving rise to these temporary differences originate in one period and reverse themselves in subsequent periods:

1. Revenues are included in taxable income *later* than in pre-tax accounting income, as when percentage of completion accounting is used in financial reports and a modified versions of this method that delays recognition of revenues is elected for tax purposes.

2. Expenses are deducted *later* in determining taxable income than in determining financial statement income, as in the case of warranty costs, which are deductible from taxable income only when incurred but must be accrued for book purposes when a sale is recognized.

3. Revenues are included *earlier* in taxable income than in pre-tax accounting income. For example, rent payments received in advance may be reported when received for tax determination, but in later periods when earned for financial reporting purposes.

4. Expenses or losses are deducted in determining taxable income *earlier* than in determining pre-tax book income, such as direct advertising expenditures that may be deducted immediately on a tax return, but amortized in the financial statement over several periods.

Temporary differences also arise when assets and liabilities acquired in business combinations have a tax bases different from their post acquisition book values.

Balance Sheet Approach

SFAS 109 is a balance sheet oriented approach to deferred tax accounting the Statement discusses deferred tax accounting primarily in terms of deferred tax assets and liabilities. Consistent with this approach, it defines periodic deferred tax expense or benefit as the net change during the period in a company's deferred tax liabilities and assets. In the case of deferred tax liabilities and assets acquired in a business transaction during an accounting period, the related deferred tax expense or benefit is the change since the combination date.

Comprehensive Approach

SFAS 109 requires the deferred tax consequences to all temporary differences to enter into the measurement of deferred liabilities and assets.

Tax credit and tax loss carryforwards are also included in the measurement of deferred tax liabilities and assets.

Valuation Allowance

Companies can become eligible for tax credits (such as a tax loss carryforward tax credit), but for one reason or another they cannot rate them for current tax obligation measurement purposes. If certain conditions are met in the future, these tax credits can still be used. These tax credits are potentially deferred tax assets.

Deferred tax assets should only be recognized in financial statements if, based on the weight of the available evidence, it is more likely than not in management's judgment that the deferred tax asset will be realized. "More likely than not" is defined in SFAS 109 as a probability of more than .5%. Deferred tax assets that are not likely to be realized are recorded off balance sheet in the so-called "valuation allowance" and disclosed in the tax note.

Management should review the adequacy of the valuation allowance at each measurement date. Any change in the valuation allowance should be included in income from continuing operations (a credit to deferred tax expense) accompanied by the appropriate entry to the deferred tax asset account (a debit to the asset).

Management should consider tax planning strategies in determining the amount of valuation allowance required. Tax planning strategies include actions that are prudent and feasible that a company might take to prevent an operating loss or tax credit carryforward from expiring unused or result in the realization of deferred tax assets.

Enacted Change in Tax Laws or Rates

Deferred tax liabilities and assets are adjusted in the period of the enactment for the effect of an enacted change in tax laws or rates. The effect is included in income from continuing operations.

Tax Allocations

The income tax expense or benefit for the accounting period must be allocated among continuing operations, discontinued operations, extraordinary items, and items charged or credited directly to owners' equity.

Exemptions

There are a number of exemptions to SFAS 109. The principal exemption is that a deferred tax liability need not be recognized for potential U.S. taxes on repatriate overseas income that will not be incurred since management does not intend to repatriate the income to the United States.

Display

In most cases deferred tax asset and liability balances are classified as current or noncurrent based on the classification of the related asset or liability for financial reporting purposes.

Financial Analysis

The tax expense note accompanying the financial statement should always be carefully analyzed by statement users. It can be a valuable source of information. Statement users should always note the following:

1. *The percentage deferred taxes are of the total tax expense.* A high percentage may suggest liberal book accounting is being used, income is being recorded that may not be realized as cash until a much later period, or the company is relying on tax-shelter schemes to protect its income from taxes.

2. *The percentage book tax expenses are of the book pre-tax income and the dollar contribution to the change in earnings attributable to the change in the book tax rate.* A reduction in the book tax rate and/or a high contribution of tax savings due to a change in income tax rate may indicate that management is becoming more reliant on tax rate management as a source of net income. A low tax rate might indicate the company is vulnerable to tax code changes or its earnings are in low tax rate environments that might have restrictions on the use of profits earned in those locations. Low tax rates are generally considered low-quality earnings sources and a possible red flag. In making these calculations, equity-method income should be excluded. It can distort the tax rate percentage as it is included in pre-tax profits on an after-tax basis.

3. *Unusual change in the tax effect of individual temporary difference items.* A significant change may indicate a change in the level of activity related to the item or a shift in book or tax accounting methods and estimates.

4. *The company's past policy toward accruing potential U.S. taxes on overseas earnings.* The nonaccrual of potential U.S. taxes that would be due on repatriated foreign earnings could expose the company to a tax expense charge in a later period when the previously recorded overseas profits are repatriated.

5. *The current portion of the tax expense.* A decline in this figure is indicative of a lower level of profits reported to taxing authorities.

6. *One-time tax savings and sources of tax savings that are vulnerable to tax code changes.* The contribution of these items to net income might be norecurring and as such should be regarded as a low-quality earnings source.

7. *Capital gains.* Taxes attributable to capital gains might indicate that the company is selling assets at a gain to cover a decline in operating earnings.

8. *Valuation allowance changes.* Management may be manipulating the deferred tax asset valuation allowance to manage earnings rather than to reflect genuine changes in the company's prospects.

How deferred taxes should be regarded in financial analyses is a controversial topic. Some analysts argue that, in most cases, deferred tax liabilities are equivalent to permanent equity capital and should be lumped with owners' equity when computing debt-to-equity ratios. Others with this same view go even further. They would exclude deferred tax expenses from income in computing return on equity. In making this calculation, these individuals, for some unexplained reason, do not add the deferred tax liability back to owners' equity. This is a mistake. Many analysts, while recognizing that deferred tax liabilities are not the equivalent of debt and deferred tax expenses are not like most expense items that must be paid in cash, accept the deferred-tax-accounting liability and expense classification for financial ratio purposes. This latter approach is generally followed when computing margin and return on investment ratio for management performance evaluation purposes. It is based on the belief that normalized earnings figures are better indicators of management performance over time than, say, income based on recognition of only the current portion of the tax expense. In contrast, in most financial structure analysis, all or some portion of the deferred tax liability is usually excluded from liabilities and/or included in equity. This treatment reflects the widespread acceptance among statement users of the quasi-equity nature of most deferred tax liabilities.

INTRODUCTION TO OWNERS' EQUITY

(W.J. Bruns, Jr. / #9-193-049 / 9 p)

Summary

An introduction to accounting for owners' equity and leveraged buyouts. Covers classes of shareholders, treasury stock, stock distributions, and dividend accounting.

Outline

Accounting for Ownership in Corporations

Classification of Owners of Corporations
Rights and Responsibilities of Shareholders
Accounting for Dividends
The Sale of Stock and Stock Distributions
Treasury Stock
Cumulative Foreign Currency Translation Adjustments

Mergers, Acquisitions and Leveraged Buyouts (LBOs)

Learning Objectives

After reading the note and completing the following exercises, managers should be able to:

- Become familiar with the various classifications of stockholders' equity on a balance sheet.
- Better understand how their company finances its activities.

Questions and Ideas to Consider

Take a look at the owners' equity section on your firm's balance sheet. How does the information in this section change the picture of your company's overall financing? For example, does your firm appear to be funding its activities through equities as well as debt? What might be the reason for that?

WILLIAM J. BRUNS

Introduction to Owners' Equity

Almost all business organizations take one of three forms. The simplest form of organization is the *proprietorship*, or the business owned by a single individual. Typically, this individual has committed personal resources to the organization and has created the business entity. Whatever success the entity enjoys accrues to the owner as an individual. A *partnership* is a somewhat more sophisticated organization form, but it maintains several attributes of a single proprietorship. In this form, two or more persons agree to pool their resources and create a business entity, the success of which they will share equally or according to some agreement between them. The third widely used form of business organization is the *corporation*. In legal form, a corporation is more complex than either a proprietorship or partnership, but it is extremely popular for several reasons. One of the most important reasons is that it allows many investors to contribute their resources to one endeavor without the complication of agreements among them individually. Under the law, a corporation is a legal entity and as such assumes its own obligations. This frees the investor from having to use personal resources above the amount originally invested to satisfy claims against the entity, limiting liability. It also allows the use of ownership shares that can be exchanged for money or other securities should the shareholder wish to divest of ownership rights.

In terms of the aggregate amount of resources controlled by business organizations, the corporation is by far the most important form. It is for this reason that the remainder of this note will be concerned with corporation owners' equity.

Accounting for Ownership in Corporations

Several technical complexities of accounting for ownership in corporations are the result of the laws that allow the creation of the corporation. The corporation must account to owners in the form required by the laws of the state or country in which the entity was formed; if securities issued by the corporation are traded publicly, regulations of applicable Company's Acts, the Securities & Exchange Commission, stock exchanges, and other regulatory agencies must also be heeded. Legal distinctions among classes of ownership, types of capital contributions, and the retention of the accumulated retained earnings are extremely important to the accountant maintaining records of corporate activity for management or public reporting. But from our point of view, they are important only insofar as some understanding is necessary if we are to read and use intelligently the accounting information in published financial reports.

Professor William J. Bruns prepared this note as the basis for class discussion.

Classification of Owners of Corporations

The owners of the common stock are the owners of the corporation. This group ultimately bears the risk of the operation of the business organization. It is also usually the last to receive distributions of income. In return for this assumption of risk not taken by others, it may receive higher returns than others if the entity is successful. It also usually has voting rights. In many respects, the common shareholder is analogous to the owner in a proprietorship.

Another important class of owners in some corporations is the preferred shareholders. The importance of the *preferred* designation usually revolves about the promise that dividends will be paid to this class of shareholders in a specified amount each period before any dividends are paid to common shareholders. Legal distinctions about payments in excess of this specified amount, or the effect of skipping a dividend payment on future dividend payments, can create a host of different legal subclassifications under the general category of preferred shareholders.

A third class of owners who may have some rights in particular situations within corporate operations, are those who hold certain classes of debt, such as mortgage bonds or debentures, which either give them a voice in the activities of the corporation or allow them to obtain a voice if certain contractual obligations are not satisfied. Some bond agreements allow holders to convert to an ownership interest at some time in the future or under specified conditions.

Rights and Responsibilities of Shareholders

The common shareholders are responsible for the management of the corporation. But due to the large number of shareholders typically represented, taking an active part in day-to-day management is usually impossible. This right is normally exercised through their election of a board of directors, which selects and directs the management of the corporation. While it is possible for shareholders to step forward and play a more active role in management by replacing those managers who have been selected by the board of directors with others, or even by replacing the board of directors itself, such action rarely occurs. Dissident shareholders are more apt to sell their interest in the corporation, thereby transferring their rights to others. They are then free to invest in situations in which they feel more comfortable, from which they feel they can receive a more satisfactory return, or through which they can accomplish other personal objectives.

It is important to note that the relationship between a corporation and common shareholders is not a direct one, but rather an indirect one through their acquisition of shares. The corporation sells shares originally in exchange for assets or services, usually cash, to shareholders. If original shareholders subsequently exchange their shares, transferring their rights to others, the corporation receives no added benefits. Records of current owners of shares are maintained by the company or its agents to ensure payment of dividends to current holders of shares. But the amount received by the corporation for a given share is determined only once—at the time the share is issued.

For many large corporations, shares are traded on a day-to-day basis on stock exchanges or through other electronic auction mechanisms. The prices for which shares are traded depend upon the evaluations and assessments of future corporate prospects by current shareholders and prospective investors. Except for those situations in which the corporation itself may acquire shares once held by shareholders (*treasury stock*), the owners' equity section in financial reports is unaffected by the day-to-day trading of ownership shares.

Accounting for Dividends

Cash or other assets are paid to shareholders as a dividend only when a dividend is declared by the board of directors. The decision to pay cash dividends normally rests on the availability of resources not essential to the continued operation of the corporation and the desire of the board of directors to provide some immediate and tangible return to those who have invested in the common shares of the corporation. A cash dividend is typically declared on a per-share basis; that is, the declaration may read "the Board of Directors of the X Corporation will pay a dividend of $.125 per share to each shareholder of record as of February 28, 1997." The effect of this declaration, which might be made at any time prior to the payment date, will be to cause a dividend check to be prepared and mailed to each owner whose name is registered as the owner of shares by the secretary or agent of the corporation. The check to each shareholder will represent the dividend payment appropriate to the number of shares owned.

At the time a dividend declaration is made, the effect on owners' equity should be apparent. A new obligation is created since the dividend declaration has a legal standing amongst the other obligations and liabilities of the corporation. Retained earnings, a part of owners' equity, is reduced, and the declared dividend becomes a liability to the corporation. The following are the journal entries when a dividend of $100,000 is declared and subsequently paid.

Date of Declaration: The date on which the Board of Directors declares the dividends.

> Dr: Retained Earnings $100,000
>   Cr: Dividends Payable $100,000

Date of Record: The date used to establish those stockholders who will receive the declared dividend. No journal entry is recorded.

Date of Payment: The date the dividend is paid to the shareholders of record.

> Dr: Dividend Payable $100,000
>   Cr: Cash $100,000

The Sale of Stock and Stock Distributions

When you examine the owners' equity section of a statement of financial position for a corporation, you are likely to find a minimum of three classifications. One of these is likely to be titled common stock; the second, paid-in-capital in excess of par or some equivalent phrase; and finally, a third, retained earnings.

Shares are typically issued by a corporation in exchange for resources, usually cash, that are given by the investor to the organization in exchange for the rights they obtain by owning shares. Usually the entire amount that an owner pays for shares is transferred to the corporation, except perhaps an amount for commissions to some selling agent for carrying out certain promotional activities related to the sales of shares. In the simplest form, sale of stock involves recognition that the resources of the organization have been increased without a related legal obligation to pay in the future. The effect of such an exchange is to increase owners' equity in the classification of common stock. However, legal distinctions required in accounting for owners' equity frequently complicate this simple procedure.

Common stock may be legally identified as par value stock or no par stock. Par value stock typically has a money figure quoted with it; that is, the corporation may be authorized to issue up to 1,000 shares of common stock with a par value of $5.00 per share. The mechanism of stated par value at one time was designed to protect investors and creditors, but today it has lost much of its significance. For this reason, many shares are now simply identified as no par common shares. However, to complicate the task of accounting for corporate equities, when no par shares are used, the laws of some countries and states require that a *stated value* per share be established, and that this be used in lieu of par value in recording the sale of shares. The use of par value or stated value means that not all the proceeds from the issuance of shares are credited to the common stock account. Those in excess of par or stated value are credited to a separate account called *paid-in-capital in excess of par* or sometimes *capital surplus*.

For example, XYZ sells 50,000 shares for $5 per share. Each share has a $1 par value. The journal entry that would be recorded is the following:

Dr: Cash	$250,000	
Cr: Common Stock		$ 50,000
Cr. Paid in Capital in Excess of Par		$200,000

Exhibit 1 shows the stockholders' equity of the Gillette Company and Subsidiary Companies at the end of 1995 and 1994. Gillette has issued a cumulative convertible preferred stock to its employee stock ownership plan; some details about this issue and its use are shown in the Notes to Consolidate Financial Statements included in **Exhibit 1**. Retained earnings are identified as *earnings reinvested in the business*. The two items shown as shareowners' equity, *treasury stock* and *cumulative foreign currency translation adjustments*, will be discussed briefly below.

Amounts of paid-in-capital and common stock are usually subjected to some restrictions under the laws of the country or state in which the corporation is incorporated. These restrictions usually prevent dividend payments to common shareholders when the net worth of the corporation is less than the sum of par or stated values.

Sometimes shares are distributed in exchange for services or for resources other than cash. The basic principles for recording ownership rights remain the same. The valuation of shares issued rests in these cases on the market value of services or resources acquired, often measured by the market value of shares given in exchange. Thus, the owners' equity, as recorded in the common stock and related paid-in-capital accounts, should give the reader of a financial statement some impression of the amount contributed by shareholders to the corporation in the form of resources or services.

In addition to the distribution of shares through sale, other means have been established for increasing the number of shares outstanding. Stock distributions can take the form of *stock splits* or *stock dividends*. While a distinction is normally made between these two types of transactions, they are essentially the same. Both can be referred to as stock distributions. (See **Exhibit 1** Notes to Consolidated Financial Statements for a description of a "100% common stock dividend" issued by the Gillette Company in 1995.)

Stock distribution takes place whenever the board of directors elects to send additional shares to each shareholder on a pro-rata basis. In the case of a stock split, no entry in the records or change to the monetary amounts is shown in the reports of the organization, except that the par value changes. A memorandum stating that the number of shares outstanding has been changed is appropriate. Accounting for stock dividends is somewhat different. Provided the stock dividend increases the number of shares outstanding by 20% or less, an amount equal to the market value of the shares distributed is transferred from retained earnings to the common stock and paid-in-capital account. Because the dividend results in the permanent transfer of retained earnings to paid-in- capital, the effect of a stock dividend transaction is sometimes referred to as *capitalizing retained earnings*.

Treasury Stock

When shares are traded on open financial markets, the corporation can purchase its own shares. Alternatively, some shareholders may express dissatisfaction with management action, and management may negotiate a purchase of the dissident shareholders' stock.

Sometimes shares are reacquired to reduce permanently the number of shares outstanding. If so, the shares are retired, and the records of their initial sale are updated to show that the shares are no longer in the shareholders' hands. Any apparent gain or loss in their cancellation affects the net worth of the remaining shares, but it has no income statement effect.

At other times, shares are reacquired and not canceled. Instead, they are held for future resale, distribution to officers or employees, used as gifts, or even to satisfy obligations to other persons or organizations. Shares so held are called *treasury shares* and reduce the amount of owners' equity shown in the accounts. Treasury shares are not an asset because the corporation cannot own itself or any part of itself. Even though the shares may have value because people may buy them at the market price, that value is not an asset, nor does it belong to the corporation and the holders of shares still outstanding. Shares held in treasury receive no dividends nor may they be voted in shareholders' meetings. Their purchase price appears as a reduction of stockholders' equity until they are resold.

Assume ABC acquires 1,000 of its own shares at $8 per share. Each share was initially sold for $5 and had a $1 par value. There are two methods to account for treasury stock: the par value method and the cost method. The cost method is more commonly used and is recorded in the following manner.

Dr: Treasury Stock $8,000
      Cr: Cash $8,000

Alternatively, the recognition of the stock repurchase using the par value method will result in the following journal entry:

Dr: Treasury Stock $1,000   (1,000 shares at $1 par value)
Dr: Paid in Capital in excess of Par $4,000   (1,000 shares * $4 excess of par)
Dr: Retained Earnings $3,000   (to balance)
      Cr: Cash $8,000

Cumulative Foreign Currency Translation Adjustments

Many corporations own subsidiaries that operate in countries other than the domicile of the parent country. When the financial statements of these foreign subsidiaries are consolidated with those of the parent company, the foreign currency must be converted to the home country currency. The conversion process is referred to as *foreign currency translation*. Because exchange rates fluctuate over time, and because of the mechanics of translation, differences between the translated value of the subsidiaries' assets and liabilities and the translated value of the subsidiaries' owners' equity can arise. In order to maintain the equality of assets and total equities, these translation differences require recognition somewhere in the financial statements. In many circumstances, it seems inappropriate to include this difference as a gain or loss in the computation of net income, since it results only from the mechanics of the translation process. For this reason, cumulative foreign currency translation gains and losses are usually excluded from the computation of net income, but a record is maintained in the shareholders' equity section of the balance sheet to allow the integrity of the statement of financial position to be maintained with assets equaling liabilities and owners' equity.

Mergers, Acquisitions and Leveraged Buyouts (LBOs)

Because a corporation is a separate entity, it is free to purchase another corporation. Sometimes such mergers occur with the approval of the acquired firm, and sometimes they do not. An unfriendly acquisition may occur when one firm acquires another by purchasing the stock of the company being acquired by paying cash or other securities to the shareholders of the targeted firm. Unfriendly acquisitions of this type are frequently called *takeovers*. In a friendly merger, managers usually agree, and terms are negotiated that allow one firm to acquire another by issuing stock of the surviving company to shareholders of the firm being acquired. In most cases, whether an acquisition or merger is friendly or unfriendly, it is undertaken in the belief that operating efficiencies in management and facilities utilization will result in performance superior to that which would have been obtained if the two firms had continued as separate entities.

A *leveraged buyout* takes place when the management of a firm elects to add debt in order to get the cash needed to buy the shares of public stockholders. Without shareholders (or at least nonmanagement shareholders), it is less likely that a corporation will be a target of an unfriendly acquisition. The burden of servicing the added debt and paying interest as it falls due affects both cash flow and profitability of the corporation.

In some cases, leveraged buyouts have taken place because a group of managers hope to leverage the performance of the corporation to their own benefit by eliminating other shareholders and by using financial leverage to the advantage of the shares they own. They hope the payoffs to themselves through share ownership and control of discretionary salaries and bonuses will justify the added risk of a heavily indebted corporation.

Summary

Owners' equity is both the measure of the residual equity of the owners and a record of the sources of that entity. Corporations may have different classes of shareholders. When they do, separate records are needed to report the differential rights and capitalization of the classes. Shares can usually be transferred from one owner to another without the consent of the corporation and without additional payment to the company. Usually shares are sold by the corporation only once. The companyh keeps records to maintain the distinction between the capital directly contributed and earnings subsequently retained.

Dividends can be paid only if assets are available for distribution to shareholders, and legal restrictions for protection of creditors are met. When dividends are declared, they become a liability of the firm. Stock dividends are not dividends at all; they merely represent an increase in the number of shares of ownership having a claim on an unchanged equity. They do, however, reduce the amount of retained earnings by transferring a measured amount of retained earnings to the common stock and paid-in-capital accounts. Stock distributions or splits, which may be used to increase or decrease the number of shares outstanding, do not affect the value of owners' equity.

In recent years, the phenomenon of leveraged buyouts (LBOs) has led to a shift in the capital structure of many firms. Managers borrow money, thus leveraging the firm, and use the cash to acquire outstanding shares. This transaction reduces the amount of stockholders' equity outstanding and, at the same time, increases the amount of debt . After such an LBO, the debt-to-equity ratio increases, often substantially. Returns to the remaining shareholders can be leveraged dramatically if the company is able to meet the interest payments on debt issued to retire the outstanding stock.

Exhibit 1 Stockholders' Equity—The Gillette Company and Subsidiary Companies (Excerpt from Consolidated Balance Sheets) ($ millions)

	December 31, 1995	December 31, 1994
Stockholders' Equity		
8.0% Cumulative Series C ESOP Convertible Preferred, without par value, Issued: 1995 – 160,701 shares; 1994 - 162,928 shares	$96.9	$98.2
Unearned ESOP compensation	(34.3)	(44.2)
Common stock, par value $1 per share		
Authorized 1,160,000,000 shares		
Issued: 1995 - 559,718,438 shares; 1994 - 558,242,410 shares	559.7	558.2
Additional paid-in capital	31.1	(1.4)
Earnings reinvested in the business	3,382.7	2,830.2
Cumulative foreign currency translation adjustments	(477.0)	(377.1)
Treasury stock, at cost:		
1995 - 115,254,353 shares; 1994 - 115,343,404 shares	(1,045.8)	(1,046.6)
Total stockholders' equity	$2,513.3	$2,017.3

Notes to Consolidated Financial Statements

Common Stock and Additional Paid-in Capital

In April 1995, stockholders voted to increase the authorized $1 par value common stock from 580 million shares to 1.16 billion shares. Accordingly, as previously authorized by the Board of Directors, the 100% common stock dividend to stockholders of record June 1, 1995, having the effect of a two-for-one split, became effective. All share information has been adjusted for this stock split.

	(Thousands of shares)			(Millions of Dollars)		
	Common Stock				Additional	
	Issued	In Treasury	Outstanding	Common Stock	Paid-in Capital	Treasury Stock
Balance at December 31, 1992	555,748	(115,410)	440,338	$555.8	$(41.0)	$(1,047.2)
Conversion of Series C ESOP Preferred Stock	---	14	14	---	.1	.1
Stock option and purchase plans	1,427	---	1,427	1.4	21.7	---
Balance at December 31, 1993	557,175	(115,396)	441,779	557.2	(19.2)	(1,047.1)
Conversion of Series C ESOP Preferred stock	--	53	53	---	.3	.5
Stock option and purchase plans	1,067	---	1,067	1.0	17.5	---
Balance at December 31, 1994	558,242	(115,343)	442,899	558.2	(1.4)	(1,046.6)
Conversion of Series C ESOP Preferred Stock	---	89	89	---	.5	.8
Stock option and purchase plans	1,476	---	1,476	1.5	32.0	---
Balance at December 31, 1995	559,718	(115,254)	444,464	$559.7	$ 31.1	$(1,045.8)

Foreign Currency Translation

Net exchange gains or losses resulting from the translation of assets and liabilities of foreign subsidiaries, except those in highly inflationary economies, are accumulated in a separate section of stockholders' equity titled, "Cumulative foreign currency translation adjustments." Also included are the effects of exchange rate changes on intercompany transactions of a long-term investment nature and transactions designated as hedges of net foreign investments.

(Millions of dollars)	1995	1994	1993
Balance at beginning of year	$(377.1)	$(415.0)	$(265.2)
Translation adjustments, including the effect of hedging	(120.4)	43.0	(154.2)
Related income tax effect	20.5	(5.1)	4.4
Balance at end of year	$(477.0)	$(733.1)	$(415.0)

Included in Other Charges are net exchange losses of $17.0 million, $77.4 million and $105.4 million for 1995, 1994 and 1993, respectively, primarily relating to subsidiaries in highly inflationary countries, principally Brazil.

Employee Stock Ownership Plan

In 1990, the Company sold to the ESOP 165,872 shares of a new issue of 8% cumulative Series C convertible preferred stock for $100 million, or $602.875 per share.

Each share of Series C stock is entitled to vote as if it were converted to common stock and is convertible into 40 common shares at $15.07188 per share. At December 31, 1995, 160,701 Series C shares were outstanding, of which 103,860 shares were allocated to employees and the remaining 56,841 shares were held in the ESOP trust for future allocations. The 160,701 Series C shares are equivalent to 6,428,054 shares of common stock, about 1.4% of the Company's outstanding voting stock.

The Series C stock is redeemable upon the occurrence of certain changes in control or other events, at the option of the Company or the holder, depending on the event, at varying prices not less than the purchase price plus accrued dividends.

The ESOP purchased the Series C shares with borrowed funds guaranteed by the Company. The ESOP loan principal and interest is being repaid on a semi-annual basis over a 10-year period by Company contributions to the ESOP and by the dividends paid on the Series C. shares.

As the ESOP loan is repaid, a corresponding amount of Series C stock held in the trust is released to participant accounts. Allocations are made quarterly to the accounts of eligible employees, generally on the basis of an equal amount per participant. In general, regular U.S. employees participate in the ESOP after completing one year of service with the Company.

The unpaid balance of this loan is reported as a liability of the Company. An unearned ESOP compensation amount is reported as an offset to the Series C share amount in the equity section.

Plan costs and activity for this plan follow.

(Millions of dollars)	1995	1994	1993
Compensation expense	$6.0	$6.4	$8.5
Cash contributions and dividends paid	14.2	13.9	15.8
Principal payments	10.3	9.2	10.3
Interest payments	3.9	4.7	5.5

SOLVING THE PUZZLE OF THE CASH FLOW STATEMENT

(J.H. Hertenstein, S.M. McKinnon / #BH013 / 8 p)

Summary

The cash flow statement provides a potential wealth of information about how a company uses its assets. Unfortunately, too many readers of financial reports gloss over this part of the document and head to the long-familiar income statement and balance sheet. They probably do this because of the comparative recency of the cash flow statement and because their business schooling did not expose them to it. Contrary to most readers' assumptions, though, the cash flow statement does not require sophisticated analysis of ratios in order to appreciate its value. This article provides a straightforward sequence of steps for tapping into the trove of information that a cash flow statement offers: 1) scanning the big picture; 2) checking the power of the cash flow engine; 3) pinpointing the good news and the bad news; and 4) putting the puzzle together. A self-test is provided so that readers can assess their ability to follow these steps and thus use the cash flow statement to generate powerful information about a firm's financial operations.

Outline

Format of the Cash Flow Statement

Step 1: Scanning the Big Picture

Step 2: Checking the Power of the Cash Flow Engine

Step 3: Pinpointing the Good News and the Bad News

Step 4: Putting the Puzzle Together

Learning Objectives

After reading the article and completing the following exercises, managers should be able to:

- Better understand the purpose of a cash flow statement.

- Become familiar with the basic elements of a cash flow statement.

- Analyze their company's cash flow statement with an eye to spotting positive and negative trends in cash management.

Questions and Ideas to Consider

1. Using the steps outlined on pages 98-101, analyze your company's cash flow statement. Jot down the observations you make for each of the four steps.

   a) What positive and negative trends do you see emerging?

   b) What items require more explanation? How will you obtain this information?

   c) How can you use what you've learned to make more effective decisions as a manager?

   d) What information would help your reports to make better decisions? Why? How will you help them to use this information?

2. As the authors suggest, use the four steps described in the article to analyze the cash flow statement in Figure 4 on page 101.

   a) Compare your observations with those listed in the Notes section on page 102. How did you do?

   b) How might the authors' observations give you additional insight into your firm's cash flow statement?

Solving The Puzzle Of The Cash Flow Statement

Julie H. Hertenstein and Sharon M. McKinnon

The cash flow statement is one of the most useful financial statements companies prepare. When analyzed in a rational, logical manner, it can illuminate a treasure trove of clues as to how a company is balancing its receivables and payables, paying for its growth, and otherwise managing its flow of funds. But many readers seem to bypass the cash flow statement and head only for the old, familiar, comfortable income statement and balance sheet—despite the fact that the cash flow statement may provide considerable information about what is really happening in a business beyond that contained in either of the other two statements.

There are several reasons why the cash flow statement may not get the attention it deserves. First, although it has been around in its present format since mid-1988, it is still considered the "new statement"; many managers were not exposed to it during their business schooling in financial analysis. If they were, they may have been taught how to prepare one but not how to interpret the story it tells.

Second, the format of the "Cash Flow from Operating Activities" section of the statement can be challenging to follow if presented in what is known as the "indirect" method. But perhaps most daunting to many is the mistaken idea that it takes a very sophisticated analysis of complicated ratios and relationships to use a cash flow statement effectively.

Contributing to this notion are numerous business journal articles that have appeared in the past decade. They promote the value of this statement when appropriate cash flow ratios are used in statistical packages, such as those used to predict bankruptcy. Present day textbooks, when not merely teaching students to prepare the statement, also concentrate on describing how ratios such as "free cash flow to net income" can be derived, but say little about what truly useful information these ratios or other information

from the cash flow statement may provide.

Analyzing this statement should not present a formidable task when reviewed in the manner we are advocating here. Instead, it will quickly become obvious that the benefits of understanding the sources and uses of a company's cash far outweigh the costs of undertaking some very straightforward analyses. Executives want to know if the cash generated by the company will be sufficient to fund their expansion strategy; stockholders want to know if the firm is generating enough cash to pay dividends; suppliers want to know if their customers will be able to pay if offered credit; investors want to evaluate future growth potential; and employees are interested in the overall viability of their employer as indicated by its ability to fund its operations. These are just a few of the valuable insights to be gained from the cash flow statement.

The method we suggest for studying this valuable statement contains several steps, with the preliminary step consisting of gaining a basic understanding of the format of the cash flow statement. Once a certain "comfort level" with the structure of the statement has been attained, individual companies' statements should be examined to gain practice in using the stepwise approach described shortly. These steps consist of:

1. scanning the big picture;
2. checking the power of the cash flow engine;
3. pinpointing the good news and the bad news; and
4. putting the puzzle together.

Pay attention, for you will be tested on your new expertise at the end of this article!

A Business Horizons tutorial.

Business Horizons Copyright © 1997 by Indiana University Kelley School of Business. For reprints, call HBS Publishing at (800) 545-7685.

Format Of The Cash Flow Statement

The cash flow statement is divided into three sections: operating activities, investing activities, and financing activities. **Figure 1** presents an example of a simple cash flow statement with the three sections delineated in bold letters. Each section shows the cash inflows and outflows associated with that type of activity.

Cash flow from operating activities shows the results of cash inflows and outflows related to the fundamental operations of the basic line or lines of business in which the company engages. For example, it includes cash receipts from the sale of goods or services and cash outflows for purchasing inventory and paying rent and taxes. You will notice it does not show these items directly. It assumes that most of these cash inflows and outflows are already summarized in the "Net Income" figure, so it starts at that figure and makes an adjustment for everything that is not a true representation of "cash in and out" in net income. This approach is the "indirect format" of presenting cash flows from operating activities and is the one chosen by most companies. The indirect format can be confusing, and a longer

explanation of "direct versus indirect" formats is provided in **Figure 2** for readers who desire more information.

Regardless of how the cash flow from operating activities section is formatted, it is important to remember that this is the most important of the three sections because it describes how cash is being generated or used by the primary activities of the company. To picture activities that affect cash flow from operations, think of the cash receipts and payments that make most working capital accounts on the balance sheet increase or decrease. For example, accounts receivable decreases when cash is collected from customers, inventory increases when goods are purchased, and accounts payable decreases when suppliers are paid for their goods.

The next section is called *cash flow from investing activities.* Here you see the cash flows associated with purchases and sales of non-current assets, such as building and equipment purchases, or sales of investments or subsidiaries. An easy way to picture what activities would be here is to think again of a balance sheet. If you assume current assets are associated with operations, then the activities associated with all the rest of the assets are in this section.

The third section is called *cash flow from financing activities.* Again, the balance sheet provides a handy way of discerning what would be in this section. If you eliminate the current liabilities associated with operations, then the activities of all the rest of the liabilities and the stockholders' equity accounts are summarized here. These are all the flows associated with financing the firm, everything from selling and paying off bonds to issuing stock and paying dividends.

Warning! There are exceptions to everything, and the cash flow statement format has a few to watch out for. Two working capital accounts, one asset and one liability, are dealt with outside the cash flow from operating activities section. Short-term marketable securities are treated as long-term investments and appear in cash flow from investing activities; similarly, short-term debt is treated as long-term debt and appears in cash flow from financing activities.

Another anomaly is the treatment of interest and dividends. Although dividends are handled as a cash outflow in the cash flow from financing activities section, interest payments are considered an operating outflow, despite the fact that both are payments to outsiders for using their money! In some countries, such as the United Kingdom, interest payments are included in the financing activities section. But in the United States, the Financial Accounting Standards Board (FASB) voted that interest payments should be in the operating activities section instead. In such a

---

Figure 1
Statement of Cash Flows

Cash Flow from Operating Activities

Net Income	xxx,xxx
Adjustments to reconcile net income to net cash provided by operating activities:	
Depreciation and amortization	xx,xxx
Changes in other accounts affecting operations:	
(Increase)/decrease in accounts receivable	x,xxx
(Increase)/decrease in inventories	x,xxx
(Increase)/decrease in prepaid expenses	x,xxx
Increase/(decrease) in accounts payable	x,xxx
Increase/(decrease) in taxes payable	x,xxx
Net cash provided by operating activities	xxx,xxx

Cash Flow from Investing Activities

Capital expenditures	(xxx,xxx)
Proceeds from sales of equipment	xx,xxx
Proceeds from sales of investments	xx,xxx
Investment in subsidiary	(xxx,xxx)
Net cash provided by (used in) investing activities	(xxx,xxx)

Cash Flow from Financing Activities

Payments of long-term debt	(xx,xxx)
Proceeds from issuance of long-term debt	xx,xxx
Proceeds from issuance of common stock	xxx,xxx
Dividends paid	(xx,xxx)
Purchase of treasury stock	(xx,xxx)
Net cash provided by (used in) financing activities	(xx,xxx)

Increase (Decrease) in Cash	**xx,xxx**

Figure 2
Cash Flow From Operating Activities: Direct and Indirect Formats

The cash flow from operating activities section of a cash flow statement can be presented using the direct format or the indirect format. The bottom line is the same, but the two begin at different points. Companies are free to choose either format.

A is an income statement, followed by (*B*) the cash flow from operating activities section for the same company presented in the two different formats.

The direct method is just like a cash tax return: how much cash came in the door for sales and how much cash went out the door for the inventory and other operating expenditures. Many believe the direct format is better, because it is easier to understand at first glimpse. However, if companies choose the direct format, they must also present a reconciliation between cash flows from operating activities and net income—which is precisely what the indirect format shows! Consequently, most firms simply choose to present the indirect format.

The indirect method starts with net income as a figure that summarizes most of the cash transactions for operating activities in a firm. However, net income also includes transactions that were not cash, so we must eliminate the non-cash transactions from the net income figure to arrive at an accurate presentation of cash flows from operating activities.

A common, typically major expense that does not involve the expenditure of any cash at all is depreciation. Depreciation is always added back to net income under the indirect method. Do not be confused by this presentation into thinking depreciation somehow provides cash. It is

A. Income Statement	
Sales.....................................	$ 412,000
Cost of goods sold...............	(265,000)
Other expenses....................	(133,000)[a]
Net income........................	$ 30,000

[a]Other expenses includes $25,000 depreciation expense.

B. Cash Flow from Operating Activities (two formats)

Direct		Indirect	
Cash received from customers	$400,000	Net Income	$30,000
Cash paid to suppliers	(260,000)	Adjustments to reconcile net income to net cash provided by operating activities:	
Cash paid to employees	(70,000)		
Other cash operating expenditures .	(30,000)		
Net cash provided by		Depreciation	25,000
operating activities	$ 40,000	Changes in other accounts affecting operations:	
		(Increase) in receivables......	(12,000)
		Decrease in inventory..........	5,000
		(Decrease) in payables	(8,000)
		Net cash provided by operating activities	$ 40,000

only added back because it was subtracted to get to net income in the first place, and it must now be added back to get to cash. If there are other expenses that did not involve cash, these too will be added back to net income.

For most income statement items, the cash paid (or received) could be a little more, or a little less, than the income statement item. For example, cash received from customers could be a little more than revenues, especially if we collected large amounts owed to us from prior years, or it could be a little less if we made significant credit sales this year. Changes in operating working capital accounts reveal whether or not the amounts included in net income for sales, inventory costs, and other expenses really reflect the actual cash inflows and outflows. Changes in these accounts are added back to or subtracted from net income to reveal the true cash inflows and outflows.

Say the total sales number on our income statement was $412,000. But if we examined accounts receivable, we would find that receivables increased by $12,000, which customers essentially "put on their bill," and only $400,000 was actually collected in cash. So the deduction of $12,000 for "increase in receivables" in the indirect format adjusts the sales number of $412,000 down to $400,000, the actual cash received.

The inventory decrease reveals that we used some inventory purchased in prior years for sales this year. Our cost of goods sold figure in net income is therefore too high as an indicator of cash paid this year for inventory.

Similarly, it looks as if we paid some of last year's bills this year, because our payables went down by $8,000. So we must subtract an additional $8,000 to adjust the net income figure for the additional, actual cash expenditures.

There is a simple rule by which accounts should be added to or subtracted from net income: *Increases in current assets are subtracted, and increases in current liabilities are added.* The simplest approach to remember this is to pick a single account that is easy to figure out when it changes in one direction. For example, you might remember that increases in accounts receivable represent goods sold on account, but not for cash; so increases in accounts receivable must be subtracted from net income to reflect cash flows from operating activities. Once you know this, you know that a decrease in accounts receivable must be treated the opposite way: it will be added. Now you can deduce the remaining working capital accounts. The asset accounts will be treated just like accounts receivable. And the liability accounts will be exactly the opposite. Once you know one working capital account, you know them all.

Although initially it takes practice to become familiar with the indirect format, you will discover that it actually shows quite a bit of useful information you might need to search for otherwise. The quickest way to find the company's total depreciation, for example, is on the cash flow statement. In addition, it directly displays the changes in the working capital accounts. If you were to use the balance sheet for this information, you would have to perform the subtraction yourself.

situation, one might have to adjust somewhat if one were trying to compare a UK company like British Petroleum to a U.S. company like Exxon.

Step 1: Scanning The Big Picture

Now, sit back with your favorite company's annual report and follow these steps to understanding its cash flow picture. You can think of this as a big puzzle exercise. All the pieces are there in the statement; your task is to put them in the proper context to form a mosaic from which a picture of the firm's cash flow health emerges. If you don't have an annual report handy, you can use **Figure 3**, which shows the cash flow statements for the Colgate-Palmolive Company for the years ending 1992, 1993, and 1994. We chose Colgate-Palmolive because it represents one of the best annual reports in the country and the positive trends are clear for illustrative purposes.

Other reports may not contain such "rosy scenarios," as you will discover shortly.

Scanning the big picture involves several substeps. The first is to place your company in context in terms of its age, industry, and size. We expect mature companies to have different cash flows from start-up companies, and service industries to look different from heavy manufacturing industries. Big corporations may experience declining cash flows in certain years, but the sheer immensity of their cash flows may ameliorate concerns, whereas the declining trend might be much more worrisome if they were small firms without such vast resources.

Colgate-Palmolive certainly qualifies as a mature company. It is huge (figures are rounded to millions), and it operates primarily in consumer product markets throughout the world. A firm like this should be involved in complex activities on a global scale. Colgate-Palmolive certainly is, but its cash flow statement is not much more complex than what one might expect from a much smaller, perhaps simpler, company.

Continue your big picture scan by flipping through the annual report to determine how management believes the year has progressed. Was it a good year? Perhaps a record-breaking year in terms of revenues or net income? Or is management explaining how the company has weathered some rough times?

A key part of the big picture scan is to look at a key summary figure of financial health—net income. If the cash flow statement has been prepared using the indirect method for operating cash flows, as Colgate-Palmolive's has, you can find this at the top of the cash flow statement. Otherwise you'll have to use the reconciliation of net income and operating cash flows that accompanies the cash flow statement, or take a peek at the income statement itself. What is the bottom line? Does it show income or losses over the past few years? Is income (or loss) growing or shrinking? Keep these points in mind as you examine the cash flows. In addition, scan the comparative numbers for the past three years for unusual items you'd like to have explained eventually.

Colgate-Palmolive shows positive net income for all three years—a promising start. The three-year trend appears to be positive, but a big drop in 1993 raises a few questions. The statement also reveals a few items that need to be checked out. In the operating activities section, what is that "cumulative effect on prior years of accounting changes" in 1993? And what are those "restructured operations"? File those away to examine later. Note any line items that are vastly different from year to year. Colgate-Palmolive has a few of those, including changes in its working capital accounts, the proceeds from issuance of debt, and its purchases of treasury stock.

Figure 3
Consolidated Statements Of Cash Flows: Colgate-Palmolive

(In millions)	1994	1993	1992
Operating Activities			
Net Income	$ 580.2	$ 189.9	$ 477.0
Adjustments to reconcile net income to cash provided by operations:			
Cumulative effect on prior years of accounting changes	---	358.2	---
Restructured operations, net	(39.1)	(77.0)	(92.0)
Depreciation and amortization (used up)	235.1	209.6	192.5
Deferred income taxes and other, net	64.7	53.6	(25.8)
Cash effects of these changes:			
(Increase) in receivables	(50.1)	(103.6)	(38.0)
(Increase)/decrease in inventories	(44.5)	31.7	28.4
(Increase)/decrease in other current assets	(7.8)	(4.6)	10.6
Increase/(decrease) in payables	90.9	52.6	(10.0)
Net cash provided by operations	829.4	710.4	542.7
Investing Activities			
Capital expenditures	- (400.8)	(364.3)	(318.5)
Payment for acquisitions	- (146.4)	(171.2)	(170.1)
Sale of securities and investments	58.4	33.8	79.9
Investments	(1.9)	(12.5)	(6.6)
Other, net	33.0	61.7	17.4
Net cash used for investing activities	(457.7)	(452.5)	(397.9)
Financing Activities			
Principal payments on debt	(88.3)	(200.8)	(250.1)
Proceeds from issuance of debt	316.4	782.1	262.6
Proceeds from outside investors	15.2	60.0	---
Dividends paid	(246.9)	(231.4)	(200.7)
Purchase of treasury stock	(357.9)	(657.2)	(20.5)
Proceeds from exercise of stock options	18.5	21.8	22.6
Net cash used for financing activities	(343.0)	(225.5)	(186.1)
Effect of exchange rate changes on cash	(2.9)	(6.2)	(9.3)
Net increase (decrease) in cash	$ 25.8	$ 26.2	$ (50.6)

Step 2: Checking The Power
Of The Cash Flow Engine

The cash flow from operating activities section is the cash flow engine of the company. When this engine is working effectively, it provides the cash flows to cover the cash needs of operations. It also provides cash necessary for routine needs, such as the replacement of worn-out equipment and the payment of dividends. There are exceptions, of course. Start-up companies, for example, usually have negative cash flows from operating activities because their cash-flow engines are not yet up to speed. Companies in cyclical industries might have negative operating cash flows in a "down" year; a company that has experienced an extensive strike could also be expected to have negative cash flow from operating activities. Although occasional years of negative cash flow from operating activities do not spell disaster, on the average we should expect it to be positive.

To check the cash flow engine, first observe whether cash flow from operating activities is greater than zero. Also check whether it is growing or shrinking. Assuming it is positive, the next question is whether or not it is adequate for important, routine expenditures. Just as we do not expect a start-up company to have positive cash flow from operating activities, we also do not expect a company still in a very rapid growth phase to generate enough cash flow from operating activities to cover the investments required to rapidly expand the firm. However, we do expect the operations of a mature company to generate enough cash to "keep the company whole." This would include the amount of investment required to replace those fixed assets that are used up, worn out, or technologically obsolete as well as cash required to pay the annual dividend shareholders have come to expect.

It is difficult to know precisely how much cash is required to keep the company's fixed assets "whole," because the cash flow statement does not separate capital expenditures for replacement and renewal from those for expansion and growth. However, the annual depreciation amount provides a very rough surrogate for the amount of fixed assets that need to be replaced each year. In periods when prices are rising, the cost to replace assets should be somewhat greater than the cost of older assets that are being depreciated. So to ensure that the firm is kept whole and is not shrinking, we should expect the portion of investing activities related to the purchase of fixed assets to exceed depreciation.

Important information about the cash flow engine is also revealed by examining the operating working capital accounts. In the Colgate-Palmolive operating activities section, these are shown under "cash effects of these changes." In a healthy, growing company, we would expect growth in operating working capital accounts such as inventory and accounts receivable as well as in accounts payable and other operating payables. Obviously there can be quite a bit of variability in working capital accounts from period to period. Streamlining a collections policy or implementing a Just-In-Time inventory system could shrink accounts receivable or inventory in a growing company. But on the average, inventories, receivables, and accounts payable usually grow in expanding companies. Beware of situations in which all working capital accounts increase net cash from operating activities. This likely would not happen randomly in a healthy, growing company. It normally results from deliberate management action and could indicate a company in such a cash flow crisis that managers have been forced to raid the working capital accounts to survive.

With these ground rules, let's check Colgate-Palmolive's cash flow engine. In all three years, cash flow from operating activities is greater than zero, reaching over $800 million in 1994. It increases steadily every year, unlike net income. Annual depreciation is in the vicinity of $200 million each year, and the yearly dividend is also around $200 million. Colgate-Palmolive's cash flow engine is not only generating enough cash to cover "keeping the company whole," it is also able to throw off around $400 million annually for growth and investment, and the amount of excess cash has been increasing each year.

This is a powerful cash flow engine. A glance at the working capital account differences indicates that receivables, other assets, and payables have grown (net) over the three years, while inventories have shrunk slightly. This picture is consistent with a global company increasing its scope through acquisitions and new product development.

Step 3: Pinpointing The Good News
And The Bad News

This step involves looking at the total cash flow statement to find where the rest of the "good news" and "bad news" lie. What you are looking for is the story the statement is trying to tell you. It will not come simply by divine revelation, but by systematic observation of the items on the statement and their trends over the years presented for your comparison.

Begin with cash flow from investing activities. What is this section trying to tell you? One systematic observation is to check whether the company is generating or using cash in its investing activities. Whereas we expect positive cash flow from operating activities, we also expect a healthy company to invest continually in more plant, equipment, land, and other fixed assets to replace the assets that have been used up or have become technologically obsolete, as well as to expand and grow. Although companies often sell assets that are no longer of use to them, they would normally purchase more capital assets than they sell. As a result, we generally expect negative cash flows from investing activities. As with operating activities, exceptions do occur, especially if the firm divests a business or subsidiary. However, watch for companies that are beginning to shrink substantially because they are generating much of their cash by selling off chunks of the business!

Colgate-Palmolive exhibits the signs of a "good news from investing activities" company. Capital expenditures are nearly 1.5 times the amount of depreciation, so they are clearly at a level well beyond that required to keep the company whole. In addition, Colgate-Palmolive makes significant expenditures for acquisitions in each year—another growth indicator. These numbers remain consistent or increase from year to year and paint a picture of a steadily growing company, with enough cash flow from operating activities to cover these expenditures and more.

Cash flows from financing activities could as easily be positive as negative in a healthy company. Moreover, they are likely to change back and forth, so finding the "good" and "bad" is more challenging. It requires viewing the cash flows from financing activities in conjunction with other information on the cash flow statement and basing your conclusions on the weight of the evidence and your own judgment. Assume a company has borrowed cash or issued stock. A "good news" scenario might be that the firm has carefully analyzed its leverage and cost of capital and chosen to finance itself through debt or equity rather than from cash from operations. Another "good news" scenario might be that a new start-up is doing well enough to issue an Initial Public Offering. On the other hand, a "bad news" scenario might be that the company has low (or negative) cash flows from operations and is being forced to generate funds from other sources. You must look at the entire package to evaluate whether your cash flows from financing are in the "good news" or "bad news" categories.

One systematic way to begin is to compare borrowing and payments on debt with each other across the years and note the trends. Colgate-Palmolive has been consistently borrowing more than it has paid back, and to a very substantial degree in 1993. Good news or bad? We have already seen the incredible amount of cash being thrown off from operations, so this increase in debt financing is probably the result of a conscious management decision and not the actions of a company desperately borrowing to survive.

Nevertheless, it might be worth another more detailed look if we wanted to consider whether continued borrowing provides a likely source of funds for future growth, or whether the firm is nearing its debt capacity.[1]

A second systematic step in uncovering the news in this section is to check the activities in the stock accounts. Colgate-Palmolive is not issuing much stock; instead, it seems to be buying back substantial amounts of treasury stock. In fact, that is the single largest use of cash outside of capital expenditures.[2] This is probably a "good news" scenario, because the company may be cashing in on what it considers a low price for its stock, or perhaps protecting itself from takeover attempts. In either event, Colgate-Palmolive appears to have sufficient cash available to make this large, non-routine investment. A little digging in the rest of the financial statements might present the whole story.

Step 4: Putting The Puzzle Together

In evaluating the cash flow statement, you are evaluating many pieces of evidence to produce an overall picture. However, it would be rare to find a company in which all of the evidence is positive, or in which all of the evidence is negative. To make a balanced evaluation, you must use both the good news and the bad news identified in each section of the statement. To reach an overall conclusion, you need to judge the relative importance of each piece of evidence and assess its relationship to the overall picture. As in a legal case, your conclusion needs to be based on the "weight of the evidence."

Before proceeding with the overall evaluation, one loose end to tie up at this point might be any unusual line items you spotted in your scan of the big picture. Sometimes these demand that you ask an expert, but frequently you can think them through or search for illumination elsewhere in the annual report. Earlier we identified two unusual line items for Colgate-Palmolive. One was the "cumulative effect on prior years of an accounting change" in 1993. Without the deduction of this $358 million item from income in 1993, Colgate-Palmolive had a healthy income figure of $548 million; but after subtracting it, income fell to $190 million. The explanation is that when Colgate-Palmolive made this accounting change, all of its effects prior to 1993 were charged to income in 1993. In reality, there was no actual expenditure of cash in 1993, which is why we added this back on the cash flow statement.[3] This is good to know, because if we ignore the accounting change and the associated charge, net income has steadily increased.

The other unusual line item was called "restructured operations," which Colgate-Palmolive subtracted from net income. This means that the cash flows associated with restructuring operations occurred in a different year from when these costs were expensed on the income statement. In all three years presented by Colgate-Palmolive, it had more cash outflows for restructuring than it expensed in the income statement.

Good news or bad news? When a company restructures some of its operations, there is both. The bad news is that there was some kind of problem that required the restructuring. The good news is that the company recognized the problem and took action it hopes will be effective. Whether the restructuring cash costs are more or less than the restructuring expense is simply a timing issue. Because expenses are recognized as soon as reasonably possible, it typically requires several years after the expense has been recorded for all of the cash costs to be incurred. Colgate-Palmolive probably recognized these restructuring expenses in prior years and this is just the anticipated cash outflows catching up with them. Moreover, the amount on the cash flow statement is declining each year.

Whether or not to chase down explanations for unusual or unknown items is a subjective call. For example, if Colgate-Palmolive's restructuring charge differences were bigger or growing, it might be worthwhile to search for more information. However, the "weight of the evidence" so far indicates that this issue is not particularly relevant in getting at the big picture. If you encounter something you do not understand, consider its materiality. If it has a major effect on cash flow from operating activities, or if it ranks as one of the major sources or uses of cash, you should probably search for an explanation. Otherwise it may be more efficient to ignore it and concentrate on the many items you know.

Now let's summarize what we've learned by examining Colgate-Palmolive's cash flow statement. First, the good news. Net income has been positive for all three years and, if we eliminate the effects of the accounting change, has been steadily increasing. Operating cash flows have also been positive for three years; they, too, have been steadily increasing. Operating cash flows have significantly exceeded the sum of depreciation and dividends, so Colgate-Palmolive is generating enough cash from operations to expand the business. The working capital accounts are growing, consistent with the expectations for a growing business. By making capital expenditures that significantly exceed depreciation, and also by making fairly large acquisitions, Colgate-Palmolive shows that it is grooming the business for the future. There are no large-scale sales of fixed assets or divestitures that indicate any downsizing or shrinking of the business. The company has increased its dividend payments annually, an expression of management's confidence in the firm's future cash-generating capability. It also has sufficient excess cash to repurchase large amounts of its stock.

Now the bad news. The presence of charges for "restructured operations" indicates that Colgate-Palmolive has experienced problems in some portions of the business. It has borrowed significantly, in excess of repayment, which could increase leverage. The repurchase of stock could indicate management concerns with possible takeovers. And acquisitions sometimes create problems for firms; it is difficult to integrate them successfully into the company's business to ensure adequate returns.

The good news in the Colgate-Palmolive cash flow story is quite compelling. The bad news is more at the level of "concerns" rather than major cash flow problems. So considering the weight of the evidence, Colgate-Palmolive appears to have a strong positive cash flow story.

Now it's your turn. The best way to learn about cash flow statements is to study some carefully using the four steps described above. You may not become an expert but you will be able to spot the big trends and important issues involved with the management of cash in most companies.

Figure 4 provides you with the opportunity to test your newfound skills. It is similar to the

---

**Figure 4
Jones Company: Statements of Cash Flows
For Year Ending December 31**

Millions of Dollars	1995	1994	1993
Cash Flow from Operating Activities			
Net income (loss)	$ (43)	$ (189)	$ (134)
Depreciation	230	271	350
(Increase) in receivables	(121)	(25)	(4)
Decrease in inventories	50	42	30
Changes in other current accounts	16	(8)	(12)
Net cash provided by operating activities	132	91	230
Cash Flow from Investing Activities			
Capital Expenditures	(200)	(260)	(300)
Disposal of plant assets	204	200	180
Disposal of business segment	134	51	---
Net cash (used in)/provided by investing activities	138	(9)	(120)
Cash Flow from Financing Activities			
Proceeds of long-term debt	200	450	215
Reductions of long-term debt	(460)	(480)	(322)
Dividends paid	---	---	(30)
Net cash used for financing activities	(260)	(30)	(137)
Increase (decrease) in cash	$10	$ 52	$ (27)

puzzles you encountered as a child in which you spot the things that are wrong with the picture. Poor Jones Company is having some rough times, as illuminated by their cash flow statements for 1993, 1994 and 1995. See how many of these troubling developments you can identify by putting together the Puzzle of the Cash Flow Statement! (Some possible answers are listed at the end of the article.[4])

Opportunities for applying your new expertise are many. As an employee curious about your company's ability to cover your paycheck, you can check out the health of cash flow from operating activities. Or suppose you are a supplier whose customer has just announced a loss for the year and you are wondering whether to continue to extend credit. An analysis of the customer's cash flow from operating activities can provide you with evidence that the firm does or does not have strong enough cash flows from operating activities to pay its bills despite losses on the income statement.

If you are a stockholder, you may be interested in whether cash flow from operating activities is large enough to invest in the capital expenditures required to keep the company whole and make it grow while still paying the dividend you have come to expect. As an executive, you might examine the cash flow statement to determine whether it is likely that all of the major sources of cash—operating activities, issuing stock, and borrowing—will be sufficient to fund a major expansion program you plan to undertake. As your expertise increases, many other useful applications may appear to you.

The information contained in a cash flow statement cannot replace the information from the traditional income statement and balance sheet. But it does provide valuable input for understanding the <u>relationships between income</u> and its <u>short- and long-term ability to generate</u> <u>cash.</u>

Notes

1. This might be the time to go looking for clues in the rest of the annual report. Where to look? A footnote on long-term debt might seem logical, but it is often almost impossible to truly understand unless you are a Chief Financial Officer. Easier and sometimes more illuminating is to do some simple ratios on the balance sheet and income statement. How has debt

changed as a percentage of total liabilities and stockholders' equity? For Colgate-Palmolive, the percentage of debt to total liabilities and stockholders' equity is quite high and has gotten higher, from 67% in 1993 to 70% in 1994. The company's income statement reveals that interest expense has almost doubled in the last year, and a quick ratio analysis of "number of times interest can be paid from income" shows a sharp decline from 7 times to about 4-1/2 times in one year. Further examination of the cash flow statement reveals that the company purchased large amounts of treasury stock. This helps explain why stockholders' equity is low in comparison to total equities, which may make that 70% debt-to-total equity ratio more understandable.

2. This contrasts with minor stock repurchases that companies typically undertake to offer stock to employees in stock option plans; in such instances, modest treasury stock repurchases are offset by modest but comparable issuances of treasury stock.

3. An accounting change is just a "paper decision"; it affects the way net income is presented, but it does not change the fundamental economic activity of the firm, so it does not affect cash receipts or cash expenditures.

4. Some possible answers are: (1) there have been losses in all three years; (2) depreciation charges have decreased; (3) capital expenditures are less than depreciation; (4) capital expenditures are less than disposals; (5) a big accounts receivable increase needs to be investigated; (6) inventories are decreasing; (7) segments of the business are being sold off; (8) the company has stopped paying dividends; (9) debt needs to be paid off with cash flow from operations; (10) there is much borrowing; (11) there is less borrowing this year. Are creditors trusting the company less?

References

Mohamed A. Rujoub, Doris M. Cook and Leon E. Hay, "Using Cash Flow Ratios To Predict Business Failures," *Journal of Managerial Issues,* Spring 1995, pp. 75-90.

"The Top 8 Reports," *Institutional Investor,* September 1995, pp. 123-129.

Julie H. Hertenstein is an associate professor of business administration at Northeastern University, Boston, Massachusetts, where **Sharon M. McKinnon** is a professor of business administration.

DIVERSITY IN ACCOUNTING PRINCIPLES: A PROBLEM, A STRATEGIC IMPERATIVE, OR A STRATEGIC OPPORTUNITY?

(W.J. Bruns, Jr. / #9-193-045 / 12 p)

Summary

An introduction to generally accepted accounting principles and their diversity. An example shows how financial reports in one firm could differ depending on accounting methods and principles selected. Presents arguments that this may be a problem, an imperative for change, or a strategic opportunity for managers.

Outline

Generally Accepted Accounting Principles

Diversity in Accounting Principles

Diversity: Strategic Imperative vs. Strategic Opportunity

Learning Objectives

After reading the note and completing the following exercises, managers should be able to:

- Understand why the use of different accounting principles poses both problems and opportunities.

- Become familiar with some examples of diverse generally accepted accounting principles.

- Know how to find out what principles are used in their company's financial reports.

Questions and Ideas to Consider

1. Do you know what key accounting principles your finance and accounting department uses to prepare financial reports? Why do you think these approaches were selected? How might you obtain this information if it is not already available to you?

2. Exhibit 1 lists several categories of financial information and some choices within each category for how that information is presented.

   a) Identify the two or three categories that are most relevant to your department or unit.

   b) For each of these categories, explain how the choice of presenting financial information directly affects your unit. Be specific about the implications of this choice.

Diversity in Accounting Principles: A Problem, a Strategic Imperative, or a Strategic Opportunity?

In our study of accounting decision making, we have been reading and discussing situations in which managers have had choices about the way in which they would report on the results of operations and the financial condition of their organizations. We have shown that managers must choose between using LIFO or FIFO in measuring and reporting on inventories, or between straight-line depreciation or accelerated depreciation in reporting on plant, property, and equipment. For almost every classification of assets, liabilities, shareholders' equity, and revenue and expenses, alternative conventions, practices, and principles exist from which managers and their accountants can choose. With such an array of methods and practices available, what is the meaning of "generally accepted accounting principles"?

Generally Accepted Accounting Principles

In general, when managers prepare reports for use by outsiders such as lenders, investors, regulatory authorities, or other interested groups, they must choose among accounting conventions, practices, and principles, which become bases for making the measurements necessary to prepare financial reports. Once a choice is made, the concept of consistency demands that similar conventions and practices be used in subsequent periods unless there is a reason that an alternative method would be preferred. We have seen how auditors refer to the use of "generally accepted" accounting principles in expressing their opinions on many financial statements prepared for the use of outsiders.

The use of the word "principles" is perhaps unfortunate, for it connotes something more basic than, in fact, most accounting principles are. Accounting principles are not fundamental truths or even necessarily rules of conduct. They are methods used in observing, measuring, and reporting, which are widely used or which have substantial, authoritative support. A generally accepted accounting principle is created whenever a method, practice, concept, or convention is widely used by those who prepare reports, or whenever an official pronouncement is made by a group such as the Financial Accounting Standards Board in the United States, the International Accounting Standards Committee, by a change to a Company's Act, or by a regulator with authority to influence reporting and securities trading.

Professor William J. Bruns, Jr. prepared this note as the basis for class discussion.

The fact that wide use leads to general acceptance in accounting principles makes it critical to understand the accounting process and the way in which it operates. In preparing and distributing their reports, managers and their accountants participate in the development of accounting principles. Through the criteria its managers adopt in deciding which measurements should be made and reported, an organization supports and advances the development of principles that may be used even more widely in the future.

The idea of a set of generally accepted accounting principles is very important historically. When there were fewer constraints on the accounting practices that could be employed by managers in preparing reports, unscrupulous entrepreneurs often took advantage of investors, creditors, and other interested groups by rendering misleading reports about income and financial position. In an effort to avert such practices, professional accountants, regulators, independent authorities, and government agencies in most countries have sought to limit the kinds of practices that fall within the guidelines that generally accepted accounting principles provide.

Nevertheless, there is no definitive list of practices and principles that are "generally accepted." It is much easier to find lists or regulations of methods or practices that are not generally accepted. This means that in spite of all the efforts to reduce diversity in reporting practices, great diversity still remains, and anyone who seeks to use financial reports has to pay close attention to the methods used by the managers and accountants who prepared them.

Unfortunately, diversity in accounting principles presents an important problem to anyone who wants to compare the economic performance or financial position of an organization at two points in time, or with that of another organization, or to some normative standard or model. To merely look at the numbers that are reported without considering the methods that lie behind them creates the risk of faulty conclusions or errors in judgment. The next section demonstrates why this is so.

Diversity in Accounting Principles

The diversity in accounting principles is so great that it would be impossible to summarize in brief form all of the concepts, methods, and procedures that are at the present time acceptable in accounting practice. It is important at least to realize how many diverse practices are acceptable and the way in which the possibilities are multiplied if combinations of different principles and practices relating to assets, liabilities, shareholders' equity, revenues, and expenses are considered. **Exhibit 1** lists some selected examples of diverse generally accepted accounting principles for presentation of financial information about important classifications.

It would be helpful if there were some normative standard against which diverse practices and their effect on financial reports might be compared. If there were a normative standard, then accounting principles producing reports that were closest to the normative standard would be preferred. By estimating the difference between a report in hand and one based on the normative standard, a financial report reader could make a judgment about the quality of information available in the financial report. In the absence of a standard, each person who seeks to use accounting information needs to create his or her own reference point. This is harder to do than it appears at first glance. Consider the simple example that follows.

How is Diversity a Problem?

Assume that two identical companies start business at the same time, and that the events and transactions in which they engage during the first year of their operations are identical. If managers of each company choose alternative accounting principles in preparing their reports, those reports may be quite different, even after only one year. **Exhibit 2** shows the statement of financial position for each of the two companies to be the same when they begin operations. **Exhibit 3** shows the events and transactions that affect both companies identically. **Exhibit 4** shows the accounting methods used by the managers of each company in reporting those identical events and transactions. **Exhibit 5** shows the statements of income and financial position that each company will prepare at the end of one year of operations. And finally, **Exhibit 6** shows how the income of the two identical companies might be reconciled.

While this example is quite simple and is obviously hypothetical, differences like these arise in actual financial reporting. Anyone who attempts to compare financial statements from two or more entities is faced with the task of identifying the accounting methods used. Then, the impact that particular methods might have had on the reports must be estimated before any comparison of the two organizations can be made. Even when examining the financial statements of a single company through time, attention must be given to possible changes in accounting principles and the impact these changes may have had before information contained in the financial reports can be used for many purposes.

Diversity: Strategic Imperative vs. Strategic Opportunity?

Financial reports are a showcase through which managers can fulfill their obligations to provide information to shareholders and other interested parties. The fact that periodic financial reporting is required shows how important the economic community and society think reporting by managers is in facilitating the free flow of capital and preventing one group from taking advantage of another because of the information available to it. It is difficult to imagine how a modern free- enterprise economy could function without a financial reporting system that is somewhat effective.

The role that financial reporting plays in a modern economy requires that managers should be trying to report about the operations and financial condition of their organizations as accurately and informatively as possible. Those who fear that managers might withhold information to use it to their own advantage would argue that some minimum set of disclosure and reporting requirements is necessary to get managers to report effectively. Whichever points of view you have about the environment in which financial reporting occurs, you must consider what managers should do if they discover that the accounting methods and principles that they are using and reporting are not the right ones, and that a change is needed.

Why might managers or an organization be using accounting methods and principles that are incorrect or ineffective? There are at least three obvious reasons. First, it may be that the initial choice of an accounting method or principle was a poor one. Since many initial choices of accounting principles or methods are made when a firm is small or when a problem is first encountered, the implications of those choices may not be obvious. As the organization grows and develops, or as its activities stabilize, it may become obvious that the method or principle initially chosen does not provide as much or as good information as an alternative might.

A second reason why managers or an organization may need to change accounting methods or principles may be because conditions have changed. The environment in which the organization is operating, or the relationships with various suppliers, investors, or financing sources, or a change in the product mix or strategy of the firm all may dictate that an alternative method or principle would be more informative than one previously employed.

A third reason why change may be necessary may be due to the actions of management itself. In developing new strategies, in taking the organization in new directions, and in adopting new tactics to deal with the action of competitors, managers may want to signal that the old accounting methods supported the old strategy, but new accounting principles and methods are needed given the chosen change in strategic direction.

Regardless of which of these three reasons creates a need for change in the accounting method or principles used in reporting, management may view the need for change as imperative. It is simply impossible to report effectively using the old method when it is obvious that a new method or principle would be more appropriate or effective.

Despite the demands for consistency that are created by the accountant's concept of consistency, an accounting change is permitted and even encouraged when it can be demonstrated that another method or principle would be preferable. In other case studies, we have seen that auditors must note a change in accounting method, but they do not need to deny an unqualified auditor's opinion simply because managers have changed accounting methods or principles. In fact, in many circumstances, the auditors append to their notice of change some phrase like "with which we concur" to signal that they are in agreement with and support the change that management has made in preparing its reports.

Unfortunately, the strategic imperative also creates the opportunity to use changes as a strategic opportunity. Selecting new accounting methods means that managers can present things differently. The results of operations or financial position can be presented in a light different than they would have been presented had the old methods or principles been retained. Because modern organizations and economic activities are so complex, what may to some managers be a strategic imperative to report things as clearly as possible, may open the door to strategic opportunities to other managers who are less scrupulous or who desire to present things in a light particularly advantageous to themselves or their organization.

Diversity in accounting principles is unlikely to be eliminated by policy, law, or practice. Diversity exists because the arena in which financial communication, accounting measurement, and financial reporting takes place is a complex one. Those who use financial reports prepared in an atmosphere where accounting diversity is the norm must examine the accounting principles and methods used, consider what alternatives might have been available, and then decide how to use the information in reports. Those who prepare financial reports and are responsible for them must consider how to balance the strategic imperative to report as accurately and honestly as possible with the strategic opportunity to present information in such a way that some who see and use the information might be misled into drawing erroneous conclusions and taking undesirable actions.

Exhibit 1   Selected Examples of Diversity in Generally Accepted Accounting Principles

Cash

1.   Include all cash on hand and in banks as one item.
2.   Use separate captions for cash on hand, and/or cash in banks, and/or cash in banks that cannot be easily withdrawn, and/or separate currencies.

Receivables

1.   Show receivables at gross amount.
2.   Show receivables at gross amount less allowances for unearned interest and doubtful accounts.
3.   Show receivables classified by type (accounts, notes, etc.), and/or by time, and/or by source (customers, employees, government, etc.).
4.   Exclude receivables unless earned and due, as in lease payments receivable.

Marketable securities (temporary investments)

1.   Show securities at cost.
2.   Show securities at market value when below cost.
3.   Show securities at cost plus interest earned but not yet paid.
4.   Show securities at approximate market value.

Inventories

1.   Show inventories at gross cost and/or by classes (supplies, raw materials, work in process, finished goods ready for sale).
2.   Show inventories at cost or market, whichever is lower.
3.   Show inventories at market or selling price.
4.   Determine "cost" or "price" by assuming average costs or standard costs.
5.   Report flow of costs and value of goods remaining by assuming last-in first-out, or first-in first-out, or average costs in and out, or standard costs in and out, etc. (Also see **Cost of goods sold** below.)

Land, plant, and equipment

1.   Show land, plant, and equipment at original cost, and/or adjusted original cost, and/or cost or market value, whichever is lower.
2.   Show plant and equipment at current value.
3.   Show plant and equipment at cost less accumulated depreciation calculated by assuming straight-line allocation of cost to periods, or by an accelerated or decelerated rate of depreciation.
4.   Charge all purchases of plant and equipment as expense in period purchased.
5.   Show land at original cost less depletion caused by mining, harvesting, or extraction of gases or fluids.

Exhibit 1 (continued)

Investments

1. Show investments in other companies at cost.
2. Show investments in other companies at cost or market value, whichever is lower.
3. Show investments in other companies at cost plus any proportional share of earnings on investment not received.
4. Show investments at market value.

Intangible assets

1. Exclude intangible assets, charging all costs related thereto as expense in the period of expenditure.
2. Show all intangible assets at cost.
3. Show intangible assets at cost but allocate costs over few periods until only a nominal value remains.
4. Show intangible assets at cost but allocate cost to all periods of expected value.
5. Show intangible assets at cost but do not charge costs to periods unless value has clearly fallen.
6. Show intangible assets at estimated value at time of acquisition, adjusted for subsequent charges.

Current liabilities

1. Show liabilities at face amount.
2. Show liabilities at amount at which obligations could be satisfied plus any costs of doing so.

Long-term liabilities

1. Show long-term liabilities at face amount.
2. Show long-term liabilities at face amount adjusted for discounts or premiums given at acceptance and amortized over period of the liability.
3. Show liabilities, including commitments on leases, pensions, and other contractual agreements, at face amount or adjusted for effects of interest.

Owners' equity

1. Show owners' equity as the amount of assets less the amount of liabilities.
2. Show owners' equity classified to show original source.

Exhibit 1   (continued)

3. Show owners' equity classified by original source but modified by transactions between the entity and shareholders, and/or extraordinary reclassifications or adjustments.
4. Within owners' equity, segregate earnings retained by implied use of resources earned.

Revenues

1. Recognize revenue in period when products or services are delivered.
2. Recognize revenue in period when product is ready for delivery (as in case of precious gems or metals).
3. Recognize revenue in period when payment is received from customer or client.

Cost of goods sold

1. Recognize expense in the period and at purchase of product delivered.
2. Recognize expense in the period and at purchase cost of some assumed unit of product delivered.
3. Recognize expense in period and at cost of replacement of the product delivered. (Also see **Inventories** above.)

Expenses

1. Recognize as expenses of the period, all or selected cash payments.
2. Recognize as expenses of the period, all expenditures related to products or services sold in the period. All expenditures are assets or in satisfaction of obligations.
3. Recognize as expenses in the period, all estimated declines in assets value and estimated increases in obligations not related to cost of goods sold.

Net income

1. Show all increases or decreases in net value of owners' equity as net income, regardless of source.
2. Exclude from net income all adjustments relating to prior periods reports, and/or extraordinary events.

Exhibit 2   Statements of Financial Position, January 1, 1992

	Company A		Company B	
Assets				
Cash		$ 500		$ 500
Marketable securities		1,000		1,000
Inventories (100 units @ $10)		1,000		1,000
Building and equipment				
(estimated life 10 years)	$2,000		$2,000	
Less: Accumulated depreciation	---		---	
		2,000		2,000
Total assets		$4,500		$4,500
Equities				
Accounts payable		$ 200		$ 200
Bank loans		1,000		1,000
Total liabilities		$1,200		$1,200
Owners' equity:				
Common Stock		3,300		3,300
Total equities		$4,500		$4,500

Exhibit 3   Events and Transactions of Companies A and B[a] for the Year 1992

Sales of merchandise (200 units @ $40 each)		$8,000
Purchase of inventory on account		
(a 3% discount is available if paid within 10 days):		
March 31	50 units @ $10	500
June 30	50 units @ $12	600
September 30	50 units @ $15	750
December 31	50 units @ $20	1,000
Paid accounts payable:		
April 30		500
July 31		600
October 31		750
Paid salaries		$2,500
Increased bank loan		$2,000
Purchased new equipment (estimated life, 4 years)		$2,000
Paid for research on new product not yet introduced		$ 500
Value of marketable securities, December 31, 1992		$ 950

[a]Assumed to be identical for each company

Exhibit 4   Accounting Methods Used In Preparing Financial Reports By Companies A and B

Item	Company A	Company B
Cash	Report face amount on hand and in bank.	Report face amount on hand and in bank.
Marketable securities	Report at cost unless market is "materially" lower and sale contemplated.	Report at lower of market cost or market.
Inventory	Report at cost, assuming first-in, first-out.	Report at cost, assuming last-in, first-out.
Buildings and equipment	Report at cost less accumulated straight-line depreciation.	Report at cost less accumulated depreciation accelerated at two times straight-line rate.
Intangible assets	Hold as asset at cost until related revenues are realized.	Charge against revenues when cash expended.
Accounts payable	Report at amount due less discounts available.	Report at face amount.
Bank loan	Report at amount due.	Report at amount due.
Owners' equity	Assets - Liabilities	Assets - Liabilities

Exhibit 5   Financial Reports of Companies A and B

Statement of Income For the Year 1992	Company A		Company B	
Sales revenues		$8,000		$8,000
Less cost of goods sold:				
Beginning inventory	$1,000		$1,000	
Add: purchases	2,850		2,850	
Available	$3,850		$3,850	
Ending inventory	1,750		1,000	
		2,100		2,850
Gross margin		$5,900		$5,150
Less expenses:				
Salaries	$2,500		$2,500	
Depreciation	700		1,400	
Research on new product	--		500	
		3,200		4,400
Operating income:		$2,700		$ 750
Add: Discount available		30		--
Less: Loss on securities held		--		50
Net Income		$2,730		$ 700

Statements of Financial Position, December 31, 1992	Company A		Company B	
Assets				
Cash		$ 3,650		$3,650
Marketable securities		1,000		950
Inventories		1,750		1,000
Building and equipment:				
Cost	$4,000		$4,000	
Accumulated depreciation	700		1,400	
		3,300		2,600
Research on new product		500		--
Total assets		$10,200		$8,200
Equities				
Accounts payable		$ 1,170		$1,200
Bank loans		3,000		3,000
Total liabilities		$ 4,170		$4,200
Owners' equity:				
Common stock		3,300		3,300
Retained earnings		2,730		700
		6,030		4,000
Total equities		$10,200		$8,200

Exhibit 5 (continued)

Statement of Cash Flows For the Year 1992	Company A	Company B
Cash from Operations:		
Net income	$ 2,730	$ 700
Add: Depreciation	700	1,400
Decrease in marketable securities	--	50
Increase in inventories	(750)	--
Increase in Accounts Payable	970	1,000
Total cash from operations	$ 3,650	$ 3,150
Cash from Inventories:		
Purchase of new equipment	($2,000)	($ 2,000)
Research on new product	(500)	--
Total cash from Inventory	($2,500)	($ 2,000)
Cash from financing:		
New bank loan	$ 2,000	$ 2,000
Total changes in cash	$ 3,150	$ 3,150
Cash, January 1, 1992	500	500
Cash, December 31, 1992	$ 3,650	$ 3,650

Exhibit 6   Reconciliation of Income for Companies A and B

Company B income	$ 700
Add $50 because Company A does not reduce value of marketable securities to market value of $950	50
Add $750 because Company A uses FIFO instead of LIFO for inventory values and determining cost of goods sold	750
Add $700 because Company A uses straight-line depreciation instead of an accelerated method	700
Add $500 because Company A retains research costs as an asset	500
Add $30 because Company A reduced liabilities to discounted amount	30
Company A income	$2,730

AUDITORS AND THEIR OPINIONS

(W.J. Bruns, Jr. / #9-197-113 / 6 p)

Summary

Discusses the purpose of independent audits of financial reports, the nature of audits and auditing, types of independent auditor opinions, and changing expectations of those who use and rely on audits.

Outline

Title and Address

Introductory Paragraph

Scope Paragraph

Opinion Paragraph

Legal Implications

Learning Objectives

After reading the note and completing the following exercises, managers should be able to:

- Become familiar with the basic elements of an auditor's report.

- Assess the auditor's report in their company's annual report.

- Understand some of the legal implications of an auditor's opinion.

Questions and Ideas to Consider

1. List the steps currently in place to help ensure that financial information from your department is accurate. What other actions could you take to increase the reliability of this information?

2. Review the auditor's report in your company's most recent annual report.

   a) Did the auditor give an unqualified opinion? If not, why not? What are the implications of an unqualified opinion for your company and for your department?

   b) Did the auditor note any changes in accounting principles used by your firm? If so, what is the significance of these changes for your unit? How will you explain their significance to your reports and colleagues?

Auditors and Their Opinions

How believable is the financial information that businesses—or any other organizations—make available to the public? There is a great deal in society that depends on this. If people are going to invest money in organizations, lend money to them, sell and buy things to and from them, even make contributions to them, they need to feel some confidence about what those organizations' resources are and how well they are being used. One job of auditors is to give people some confidence about financial information.

Making organizations' financial information believable is accomplished in different countries in different ways—with varying degrees of success. In the United States the primary mechanism for this was established in the aftermath of the stock market crash of 1929: Congress passed securities laws requiring almost all businesses whose stock is publicly traded to file with a governmental agency, on a regular basis, financial statements that have been examined by an independent auditor. These securities laws also gave that governmental agency (the Securities and Exchange Commission, or SEC) the authority to set accounting standards—that is, the way in which organizations' financial information is reported. For the most part, the SEC has outsourced this work of standard-setting to a nonprofit organization in the private sector, but it retains ultimate oversight over it.[1]

There is a very serious social purpose behind all this—to reduce "information risk" and thus promote the efficient allocation of resources in society. No one knows whether a given business or organization is going to do well or badly in the future, but if people don't have reasonably believable information about an organization in the first place, they are not going to be able to allocate resources very well. At the very least, they will—if they want to invest in a business, for example—demand a "risk premium." Thus, setting up certain information rules and requirements ultimately reduces the risk premium that businesses have to pay and lowers their overall cost of capital.

Auditors express an "opinion" about whether an organization's financial statements present a fair picture of what is going on financially in that organization. The wording of their report is prescribed by a formal "statement of auditing standards" (published by the American Institute of Certified Public Accountants). An example is shown in **Exhibit 1**. The wording of the report may, on its surface, appear fairly bland and innocuous, but it is really a distillation of a great deal of thinking and history, with individual words chosen with great care--analogous to the wording of certain

---

[1] Many organizations, both for-profit and not-for-profit, that are not legally required to have their financial statements audited do so nevertheless because potential investors, creditors, or vendors demand it.

Research Associate Jeremy Cott prepared this case under the supervision of Professor William J. Bruns as the basis for class discussion rather than to illustrate either effective or ineffective handling of an administrative situation.

statutes or contracts. There is a lot riding on the auditor's report, including the assumption of legal responsibility.

Title and Address

The title of the report always includes the word "independent." This is meant to convey that the report is coming not from the company's managers but from accountants who are independent of them and who therefore wouldn't (presumably) be biased in what they say or do not say. (If, for example, an auditor owned some of the company's stock or held a seat on its Board of Directors, that person wouldn't be considered "independent."[2]) It has become customary, in fact, for the Board of Directors of a public corporation to assign the responsibility for hiring the auditors and responding to any concerns they may have to a special "audit committee," consisting entirely of outside directors. This is meant to provide even greater assurance of the auditors' independence, to provide a "buffer" between them and management. Moreover, the auditor's report is addressed not to the company's management but to its Board of Directors and stockholders.

The independent auditor's report contains three main sections: an *Introductory Paragraph*, which indicates the degree of responsibility that the auditor is taking; a *Scope Paragraph*, which indicates the scope of the auditor's work; and an *Opinion Paragraph*, which expresses the auditor's opinion about the validity of the financial statements in question.

Introductory Paragraph

This indicates who is responsible for what. The company is responsible for preparing the financial statements; the auditor is not. The auditor is carrying out more of an oversight function and is expressing an "opinion" about what people in the company have done. Furthermore, the auditor's report covers only the financial statements (and the related notes that are, as is often said, "an integral part of the financial statements"). But a company's Annual Report often contains much more than financial statements—for example, a letter from the Chief Executive, President, or Chairperson of the Board of Directors to stockholders; management's "discussion and analysis" of results; information about stock prices—and the audit has nothing to do with those other things.

Scope Paragraph

This indicates essentially what the auditor has done. A few words in the paragraph are really loaded:

- The audit is designed to obtain "reasonable" assurance, but not absolute assurance.

- The audit examines evidence on a "test basis," but not on a comprehensive basis. That is, it relies on a statistical sampling of the data; it doesn't examine every transaction and amount.

- The audit is designed to search for "material" misstatements, but not misstatements that are immaterial. What does "material" mean? Something that "matters," in a relative sense. For example, $10,000 may be material for a small business but completely immaterial for General Motors. The nature of an item is also a factor: a misstatement of $1,000,000 in a company's Cash balance is far

---

[2] These are the expectations in the United States. In some other countries, however, an auditor may sit on a company's Board of Directors or own some of the company's stock.

more significant than a misstatement of $1,000,000 in the balance of Accumulated Depreciation. Auditing standards are ultimately quite practical in suggesting what is material: something is "material" if it is significant enough to influence the decision of a reasonable user of the financial statements (e.g., an investor or creditor or regulatory agency).

The implicit decision of society, reflected in the scope paragraph, is that there are costs as well as benefits to information and that an auditor can do only so much. What goes on in most public corporations is complicated. To require auditors to examine every financial transaction and amount—even if it were possible to do so—would cost too much, and investors wouldn't pay for it. The audit can provide only "reasonable assurance" of the validity of a company's financial statements. But that nevertheless represents a great deal: a company cannot give out whatever financial information it wants to in whatever form it wants. There are standards against which its financial information will be judged.

Opinion Paragraph

The opinion paragraph typically consists of only one sentence. It is the most important part of the report, however, and, for that reason, the entire report is sometimes referred to as "the auditor's opinion."

The sentence begins "In our opinion...." This means that the auditor is reasonably sure of his or her conclusions. Earlier in the century, the typical auditor's report "certified" the company's financial statements as being "correct." That kind of language was eventually dropped, however, because it gave the reader the incorrect impression that things could be measured exactly and without any ambiguity. The auditor's opinion is an informed opinion, and it is extremely serious, but—like a doctor's opinion—it involves an exercise of judgment and doesn't provide any guarantees.

The key issue is whether the company's financial statements conform with "generally accepted accounting principles" (often referred to as "GAAP" in both the general business press and the accounting profession). What *are* "generally accepted accounting principles"? In fact, there isn't any official, definitive list of them. In the United States, the SEC has the legal authority to specify acceptable accounting practices, and, for the most part, it has delegated that authority to a nonprofit organization in the private sector.[3] What that organization says, however, is supplemented by the pronouncements and interpretations of various other professional organizations as well as by practices that become commonly accepted within certain industries. Thus when an auditor decides whether or not a company's financial statements conform with "generally accepted accounting principles," that person not only has to consider a certain amount of ambiguity in the principles themselves but also has to exercise judgment about how general principles apply to very specific situations. It is not a straightforward task.

The report shown in **Exhibit 1** is the standard auditor's report. It represents an "unqualified" opinion (sometimes called a "clean" opinion). This is what a company wants. The report is saying essentially that the *quality* of the financial statements is fine (that is, they conform with GAAP), and there has been no problem with the *scope* of the audit (that is, nothing has prevented the auditors from gathering the evidence needed to support their opinion).

---

[3] Since 1973, the organization that has been primarily responsible for issuing accounting standards for the private sector (both for-profit and not-for-profit organizations) is the Financial Accounting Standards Board (FASB), located in Norwalk, Connecticut. To date, it has issued over 120 "Statements of Financial Accounting Standards." Another organization, called the Government Accounting Standards Board (or GASB) issues accounting standards for the public sector (that is, governmental entities).

Sometimes the auditors will add some explanatory language to their report, even when they are expressing an unqualified opinion. This is a way of drawing attention to some special circumstance—for example, if part of the audit was carried out by other auditors, or if a legitimate change in accounting principles has occurred.

There are, however, three serious *exceptions* to an unqualified report:

- *Qualified opinion.* This means that the financial statements contain some "material" departure from GAAP, or that there has been some "material" limitation placed on the scope of the auditors' work, but these problems do not overshadow the *overall* fairness of the statements. For example, a significant misstatement in the value of fixed assets might affect someone's willingness to lend money to the company if the assets were to be used as collateral, but the overall financial picture given of the company might still be fair. The wording of a qualified opinion would be similar to that of an unqualified opinion but would add the phrase "except for" and a brief explanation of what the problem is.

- *Adverse opinion.* This is more serious. This means that the financial statements contain departures from GAAP that are so material or so pervasive that the financial statements as a whole are misleading.

- *Disclaimer of opinion.* This means that the limitations placed on the scope of the auditors' work have been so material or so pervasive that the auditors simply do not have an adequate basis for expressing an opinion.

In practice, adverse opinions are rare because they would be of virtually no use to the client: potential investors wouldn't invest in the company, and potential lenders wouldn't lend money to the company. If auditors feel that a client's financial statements contain such material departures from GAAP as to warrant an adverse opinion, this situation would be discussed with the company's audit committee or management, and management would probably agree to make the necessary changes because not doing so would carry intolerable implications. Auditing standards, moreover, prohibit auditors from sidestepping an adverse opinion by disclaiming an opinion.

Legal Implications

What, however, happens in the real world? In the real world, auditors' opinions have come under increasing scrutiny and have provoked a good deal of litigation and scandal. Even harsh critics of the auditing profession in the United States acknowledge that, in the vast majority of cases, auditors' opinions are reliable.[4] In the 1980s and 1990s, however, there has been an enormous number of business failures, most significantly in the savings and loan industry, and many people—including some members of Congress—believe that auditors have not provided adequate warning to the public. People are astonished to see businesses file for bankruptcy not long after their auditors gave them a "clean" opinion. As a result, auditors in the United States have faced literally billions of dollars in damage claims.

Defenders of the profession regard many of the lawsuits as unjustified: when businesses fail, the auditors are sometimes seen as the only party left with "deep pockets," and investors and creditors may try to recoup their losses any way they can.

On the other hand, there clearly have been problems with the way in which auditors go about their work. A study by the federal government's General Accounting Office found that the audits of

---

[4] Mark Stevens, *The Big Six: The Selling Out of America's Top Accounting Firms* (Simon & Schuster, 1991), p. 254.

more than half of a sample number of bankrupt savings and loans failed "to meet professional standards." The National Commission on Fraudulent Financial Reporting, staffed by representatives of major accounting organizations, acknowledged that revenue and profit pressures in the auditing firms themselves detracted from the quality of their audits. The fact is that, even though auditing firms have a responsibility to provide independent judgments about the believability of organizations' financial information—to be, in effect, a guardian of the public interest—they also have a private interest in making money. Naturally, they want to retain clients; they don't want to offend them. "As all accounting firms are well aware, clients determined to have their way on critical issues will often shop for the 'right' audit opinion, using the competition among the firms to find a 'cooperative' auditor. Those that fail to cooperate often lose the business."[5]

In response, expectations have been formally raised. Auditors used to be required to plan their search for material misstatements "within the limitations of the audit process."[6] Now, they are required to be more pro-active: auditors have to provide "reasonable assurance" of detecting material misstatement based on a documented assessment of specific risk factors for misstatement.[7] They first set up an audit plan, but if the risks of material misstatement appear to be greater than anticipated, they have to modify the plan. They may even have to modify it several times. A similar change has occurred regarding the possibility of bankruptcy. Auditors used to assume that their clients had the ability to continue as a "going concern."[8] Now, they are required to be more pro-active on this issue as well.[9]

Finally, auditors used to assume that their clients were honest,[10] even though they were expected to carry out their work with an attitude of "professional skepticism." Now they are expected to assume that their clients are neither honest nor dishonest.[11]

---

[5] Ibid., p. 87.

[6] Statement of Auditing Standards 16 (effective in 1977).

[7] Statements of Auditing Standards 53 and 58 (effective in 1989) and 82 (effective in 1997). The second sentence of the "Scope Paragraph" in **Exhibit 1** ("[Generally accepted auditing standards] require that we plan and perform the audit to obtain reasonable assurance about whether the financial statements are free of material misstatement") is new to the standard auditor's report (as of 1989). The previous version of the standard auditor's report (in use since the late 1940s) contained no such assertion.

[8] Statement of Auditing Standards 34 (effective 1981).

[9] Statement of Auditing Standards 59 (effective 1989).

[10] Stevens, op. cit., p. 60.

[11] Statement of Auditing Standards 53 (effective in 1989).

Exhibit 1

Standard Auditor's Report

[Title]

Report of Independent Auditors

[Addressed to:]

Board of Directors and Stockholders

of XYZ Corporation

[Introductory Paragraph}

We have audited the accompanying balance sheets of XYZ Company as of June 30, 1997 and 1996, and the related statements of income, retained earnings, and cash flows for the fiscal years then ended. These financial statements are the responsibility of the Company's management. Our responsibility is to express an opinion on these financial statements based on our audits.

[Scope Paragraph]

We conducted our audits in accordance with generally accepted auditing standards. Those standards require that we plan and perform the audit to obtain reasonable assurance about whether the financial statements are free of material misstatement. An audit includes examining, on a test basis, evidence supporting the amounts and disclosures in the financial statements. An audit also includes assessing the accounting principles used and significant estimates made by management, as well as evaluating the overall financial statement presentation. We believe that our audits provide a reasonable basis for our opinion.

[Opinion Paragraph]

In our opinion, the financial statements referred to above present fairly, in all material respects, the consolidated financial position of XYZ Company as of June 30, 1997 and 1996, and the results of its operations and its cash flows for the years then ended in conformity with generally accepted accounting principles.

R. Smith & Co.

Certified Public Accountants

August 15, 1997

Source: Statement of Auditing Standards 58 (effective in 1989).

INTRODUCTION TO FINANCIAL RATIOS AND FINANCIAL STATEMENT ANALYSIS

(W.J. Bruns, Jr. / #9-193-029 / 15 p)

Summary

Introduces and describes meaning and uses for financial ratios to assess profitability, activity, solvency and leverage, and returns to shareholders.

Outline

Profitability Ratios

Activity Ratios

Solvency and Leverage Ratios

Market-related and Dividend Ratios

Using Ratios to Think about Management Strategies

Common Size Financial Statements

Learning Objectives

After reading the note and completing the following exercises, managers should be able to:

- Become familiar with several types of financial ratios and their uses.

- Grasp some of the limitations of financial ratios.

- Use several common financial ratios to compare their company's performance with that of a close competitor and with industry norms.

Questions and Ideas to Consider

(In order to complete this exercise, you will need access to the annual report of your company's closest competitor, and to a resource to check industry norms for financial ratios. You should also bear in mind the author's caveat that ratios cannot give a complete picture of a company's financial health.)

Using your company's most recent financial statements, calculate one or two ratios from each of the four categories of financial ratios explained in the note.

- How do these ratios compare with the norms for your industry? What does this comparison indicate about how efficiently your firm utilizes its resources? What might account for significant differences between your company's financial ratios and industry norms?

- Calculate the same ratios from your closest competitor's annual report. How do your ratios compare with your competitor's ratios? What might account for any significant differences? What implications do these differences have for your department or unit? If your company lags behind your competitor on some key ratios, what actions could your unit take to help improve your firm's situation?

Introduction to Financial Ratios and Financial Statement Analysis

There is almost always a reason why someone picks up a set of an organization's financial statements and begins to analyze it. Lenders or creditors may be interested in determining whether they will be repaid money they have lent or may lend to the organization. Investors may be interested in comparing a potential investment in one organization with that of another. Employees may want to compare the current performance or financial status of their employer with earlier periods. Regulatory agencies often need to assess organizational or industry financial health and performance. Financial analysis is always based on a set of questions, and the specific questions requiring answers depend on who the financial statement user is and the reasons for his or her analysis.

Financial analyses based on accounting information consistently involve comparisons. Amounts or ratios may be compared with industry norms, the same measurement in a prior period, the same measurement in a competitor's organization, or with planned and budgeted amounts previously established. Figuring out which comparisons will best answer the questions motivating the analysis is one of the necessary steps in making the best use of accounting information.

Financial ratios can help describe the financial condition of an organization, the efficiency of its activities, its comparable profitability, and the perception of investors as expressed by their behavior in financial markets. Ratios often permit an analyst or decision maker to piece together a story about where an organization has come from, its current condition, and its possible future. In most cases, the story is incomplete, and important questions may remain unanswered.

Even though the analyst or decision maker is better informed as a result of doing the ratio analysis, the indiscriminate use of financial ratios can be extremely dangerous. Decision rules that rely on a specific or minimum value of a ratio can easily lead to missed opportunities or losses. Even the best ratio is not always indicative of the health, status, or performance of an organization. Ratios between apparently similar measurements in financial statements may be affected by differences in accounting classifications or by deliberate manipulation.

The ease with which ratios can be manipulated and the danger in using them as criteria lead many analysts to concentrate on trends in ratio measurements rather than on the absolute value or proportion expressed by the ratio itself. When a trend in the value of a ratio between financial attributes is observed, questions can be raised about why the trend is occurring. The answers to such questions provide new information, not necessarily contained in financial reports, but perhaps highly relevant and useful to the decision maker and the problem at hand.

Professor William J. Bruns, Jr., prepared this note as the basis for class discussion.

Similarly, comparisons of firms only on the basis of ratios can lead to erroneous conclusions. The diversity inherent in available accounting practices and principles can lead to differences in ratios between organizations being compared. Comparisons between companies can be made, but they must be made with care and with full attention to the underlying differences in basic accounting methods used in the reports as well as in the companies themselves. With these cautions in mind, we can proceed to examine briefly some commonly used financial ratios.

Profitability Ratios

Profitability ratios seek to associate the amount of income earned with either the amount of resources used or the amount of activity taken place. These correspond to efficiency measures often used in economic and engineering theory. Ideally, the firm should produce as much income as possible with a given amount of resources or a satisfactory amount of income using as few resources as possible.

Return on Investment (ROI)

Dividing net income by the amount of investment expresses the idea of economic efficiency. Return on assets (ROA), return on investment capital (ROIC), and return on owners' equity (ROE) are all used in financial analysis as measures of the effectiveness with which assets have been employed.

Return on assets (ROA) relates net income to the investment in all of the financial resources at the command of management. It is most useful as a measure of the effectiveness of resource utilization without regard to how those resources have been obtained and financed. The formula for this ratio is:

$$\text{Return on Assets (ROA)} = \frac{\text{Income}}{\text{Assets}}$$

The consolidated statement of earnings, consolidated balanced sheets, and consolidated statements of cash flows for the Gillette Company and Subsidiary Companies (hereafter the Gillette Company) are shown in **Exhibit 1**. These financial statements will be used as a basis for illustrating the calculation of each financial ratio in this note. For 1995, return on assets for the Gillette Company was:

$$\text{Return on Assets (ROA)} = \frac{\$823.5}{\$6,340.3} = 13.0\%$$

Return on invested capital (ROIC) relates all net income to all resources committed to the firm for long periods of time. It is calculated by dividing net income by the total amount of noncurrent liabilities and shareowners' equity. The formula for this ratio is:

$$\text{Return on Invested Capital (ROIC)} = \frac{\text{Net Income}}{\substack{\text{Total Liabilities and} \\ \text{Shareholder's Equity} \\ \text{- Current Liabilities}}}$$

Return on invested capital in 1995 for the Gillette Company was:

$$\text{Return on Invested Capital} = \frac{\$823.5}{\$6,340.3 - \$2,124.0} = 19.5\%$$

Two variations in these two ratios are often observed. Because their purpose is to compare how efficiently a pool of capital has been used—a pool that includes long-term debt as well as shareholders' equity—the after tax interest expense is often added back to income in the numerator. This can be easily calculated by the formula:

$$\text{Interest expense} \times (1 - \text{tax rate}) = \text{After tax interest expense}$$

The amount of the adjustment is the *net* interest cost. Interest expense is tax deductible, and the formula calculates the after tax interest expense by multiplying the total interest expense by the complement of the tax rate. The rationale for this adjustment is that it is a better measure of the income flow generated by management, considering all of the sources of long-term financing it has chosen to use. Without the adjustment, the income understates the earnings generated by the total pool of capital.

A second variation is appropriate when the amount of assets or invested capital is changing. Since income is earned over a period of time, the appropriate denominator in the two ratios above is probably *average* assets or *average* invested capital. This is easily approximated by adding the beginning and ending measurements together and dividing by two. The analyst has to decide if these refinements to the ratios will improve his or her ability to answer the questions at hand.

Return on equity (ROE) relates net income to the amount invested by shareholders. It is a measure of the efficiency with which the shareholders' investment through their original capital contributions and earnings retained in the business have been used. The formula for this ratio is:

$$\text{Return on Equity} = \frac{\text{Net Income}}{\text{Shareowners' Equity}}$$

Return on equity in 1995 for the Gillette Company was:

$$\text{Return on Equity} = \frac{\$823.5}{\$2,513.3} = 32.8\%$$

Note that for this ratio shareowners' equity *is* the correct denominator because the ratio is an attempt to understand what the investment by the owners alone has earned.

Earnings per Share (EPS)

Because corporations have many owners, not all of whom own an equal number of shares, it is quite common to express earnings of a company on a per-share basis for those who wish to calculate their proportional share of earnings. The calculation of earnings per share can be complicated if there is more than one class of ownership, each with differing claims against the income of the firm. Preferred stock or other securities that are convertible into common shares are often treated as common stock equivalents in making this calculation. In published financial reports, this ratio is required to be presented, often in several variations such as "primary" or "fully diluted" (a very conservative form) EPS. Although the actual formulas for EPS are usually very complex, a simplified formula showing the basic common elements is:

$$\text{Earnings per Share (EPS)} = \frac{\text{Net Income - Preferred Stock Dividends}}{\text{Number of Shares of}}$$
$$\text{Common Stock + Equivalents}$$

Net earnings per share for the Gillette Company for 1995 were $1.85.

Profit Margin

This ratio, which gives a rate of return on sales, relates two statement of income measurements to each other. For this reason, it is not a measure of efficiency, but instead, gives some indication of the sensitivity of income to price changes or changes in cost structure. The formula for this ratio is:

$$\text{Profit Margin} = \frac{\text{Net Income}}{\text{Net Sales}}$$

It is important to note that neither a high nor low profit margin necessarily means good performance. A company with a high profit margin but high investment may not be returning a great amount to investors. A firm with a very low profit margin may have required only a very small investment so that it proves highly profitable to those who invest in it.

The profit margin in 1995 for Gillette was:

$$\text{Profit Margin} = \frac{\$823.5}{\$6,794.7} = 12.1\%$$

Activity Ratios

Activity ratios provide an indication of how well assets are utilized by the organization. Efficiency in using assets minimizes the need for investment by lenders or owners. Activity ratios provide measurements of how well assets or capital are being utilized.

Asset Turnover

This ratio measures the company's effectiveness in utilizing all of its assets. The formula for this ratio is:

$$\text{Asset Turnover} = \frac{\text{Net Sales}}{\text{Total Assets}}$$

For the Gillette Company in 1995, the asset turnover was:

$$\text{Asset Turnover} = \frac{\$6,794.7}{\$6,340.3} = 1.1x$$

Since different industries require very different asset structures, comparing asset turnover ratios from one industry to those in another is potentially meaningless and must be done with caution. Likewise, when an organization participates in many industries, the exact meaning of an asset turnover ratio can be obscured, and the most valid comparisons of an asset turnover ratio at one date may be to that of the same firm at another recent date.

Asset turnover ratios can be calculated for any group of assets. Accounts receivable, inventory, and total working capital are all asset classifications for which comparison of turnover is potentially interesting and important.

Days' Receivables

Evidence about the amount of time that lapses between sales and receipt of payment from customers can be important information about the financial structure of a company. An approximation of the number of days that elapse can be obtained by dividing the amount of accounts receivable (and notes receivable if these are related to customer accounts) by the average day's sales. In cases where cash sales are a significant portion of the total, the amount of charge sales must be estimated for use in judging the length of collection.

The collection period for accounts receivable can be calculated by first dividing net sales by 365 days to determine average sales per day.

$$\text{Average Day's Sales} = \frac{\text{Net Sales}}{365}$$

Then calculate the collection period using the following formula:

$$\text{Day's Receivables} = \frac{\text{Accounts Receivable}}{\text{Average Day's Sales}}$$

Days' receivables in 1995 for the Gillette Company was:

$$\text{Average Day's Sales} = \frac{\$6,794.7}{365} = \$18.6 \text{ million}$$

$$\text{Day's Receivables} = \frac{\$1,659.5}{\$18.6} = 89 \text{ days}$$

Inventory Turnover

Determining the number of times that inventory is sold during the year provides some measure of its liquidity and the ability of the company to convert inventories to cash quickly if that were to become necessary. When turnover is slow, it may indicate that inventories are not a liquid asset and suggest they should be excluded from that category for analytical purposes. On the other hand, when turnover is quite rapid, that is when inventory is sold several times each year, the liquid character of inventory can provide funds if needed in the short term and may protect the firm against inventory obsolescence.

Inventory turnover is calculated by dividing the cost of goods sold by the inventory cost. The average inventory for the year should be calculated or approximated if there has been a significant change in inventory cost from the beginning to the end of the period. Usually it is sufficient simply to add the beginning and ending inventory amounts and to use one-half of that total as the average inventory for the year. Once the inventory turnover is determined, it can be converted to days' inventory by dividing inventory turnover into 365 days.

$$\text{Inventory Turnover} = \frac{\text{Cost of Goods Sold}}{\text{Average Inventory}}$$

$$\text{Inventory Turnover Period in Days} = \frac{365}{\text{Inventory Turnover}}$$

In some financial reports issued for shareholders, the cost of goods sold is not revealed. In these cases, it is necessary to use sales as the numerator of the ratio, which gives the appearance of providing faster inventory turnover. If the relationship between price and cost does not change, the trend in turnover period would be approximately the same between two periods. Nevertheless, it is wise to use the ratio of sales to inventory with somewhat greater care.

Inventory turnover in 1995 for the Gillette Company was:

$$\text{Inventory Turnover} = \frac{\$2,540.2}{(\$1,035.1 + \$941.2) \div 2} = 2.6x$$

$$\text{Day's Inventory} = \frac{365}{2.6x} = 140 \text{ days}$$

Working Capital Turnover

Working capital turnover is a measure of the speed with which funds are provided by current assets to satisfy current liabilities. The formula for this ratio is:

$$\text{Working Capital Turnover} = \frac{\text{Net Sales}}{\text{Average Current Assets} - \text{Average Current Liabilities}}$$

Working capital turnover in 1995 for the Gillette Company was:

$$\text{Working Capital Turnover} = \frac{\$6,794.7}{(\$2,902.4 - \$1,930.1)} = 7.0x$$

Solvency and Leverage Ratios

When an organization is unable to meet its financial obligations it is said to be insolvent. Because insolvency leads to organizational distress, or even to bankruptcy or organization extinction, ratios to test solvency are often used by investors and creditors. By measuring a company's ability to meet its financial obligations as they become current, solvency ratios give an indication of the liquidity of the company.

Current Ratio

This ratio is commonly used for testing liquidity or solvency. The formula for this ratio is:

$$\text{Current Ratio} = \frac{\text{Current Assets}}{\text{Current Liabilities}}$$

The size of the current ratio that a healthy company needs to maintain is dependent upon the relationship between inflows of cash and the demands for cash payments. A company that has a continuous inflow of cash or other liquid assets, such as a public utility or taxi company, may be able to meet currently maturing obligations easily despite the fact that its current ratio may be small. On the other hand, the manufacturing firm with a long product development and manufacturing cycle may need to maintain a larger current ratio.

The current ratio at the end of 1995 for the Gillette Company was:

$$\text{Current Ratio} = \frac{\$3,104.5}{\$2,124.0} = 1.46$$

Acid Test Ratio

In cases where there is a desire or a need to confirm the absolute liquidity of an organization, the current ratio is modified by eliminating from current assets all that can not be liquidated on very short notice. Typically then, this ratio consists of the ratio of so-called "quick" assets (cash, marketable security, and some forms of accounts receivable) to current liabilities.

$$\text{Acid Test Ratio} = \frac{\text{Quick Assets}}{\text{Current Liabilities}}$$

For 1995, add the cash, short-term investments, and receivables to calculate the acid test ratio for the Gillette Company.

$$\text{Acid Test Ratio} = \frac{\$1,709.0}{\$2,124.0} = .80$$

Debt Ratio

The degree to which the activities of a company are supported by liabilities and long-term debt as opposed to owner contributions is referred to as *leverage*. A firm that has a high proportion of debt to shareholder contributions would be referred to as being highly leveraged. The advantage to the owners of the firm of having high debt is that profits earned after payment of interest accrue to a smaller group of owners. On the other hand, when a firm is highly leveraged, risk rises when profits and cash flows fall. A company can be forced to the point of insolvency by the cost of interest on the debt.

The debt ratio is widely used in financial analysis because it reveals the effect of financial leverage. The debt ratio is calculated in different ways, and we will illustrate two here. First,

$$\text{Debt Ratio} = \frac{\text{Total Debt}}{\text{Total Assets}}$$

Alternatively, the debt to equity ratio is sometimes calculated by dividing total liabilities by the amount of shareholders' equity. The formula for this ratio would be:

$$\text{Debt - to - Equity Ratio} = \frac{\text{Total Liabilities}}{\text{Owners' Equity}}$$

Care must be taken in interpreting either of these ratios because there is no absolute level that can be referred to as being better than another. In general, as the ratio increases in size, returns to owners are higher but so also is risk higher. The trend in this ratio may reveal important management decisions about the financing of activities comparing two organizations. Differences in the size of the ratio may reveal management attitude toward risks and alternative strategies toward financing the activities of the respective entities.

Using the second of the two formulas above, the 1995 debt to equity ratio for the Gillette Company was:

$$\text{Debt - to - Equity Ratio} = \frac{\$6,340.3 \ - \ \$2,513.3}{\$2,513.3} = 1.52$$

Times Interest Earned

Almost every firm has continuing commitments that must be met by future flows if the company is to remain solvent. Interest payments are an example of such commitments. The common ratio that measures the ability of a company to meet its interest payments is times interest earned. The formula for this ratio is:

$$\text{Times Interest Earned} = \frac{\text{Pretax Operating Income} \ + \ \text{Interest Expense}}{\text{Interest}}$$

The number of times interest payments are covered by current earnings offers some measure of the degree to which income could fall without causing insolvency in this account. In many cases, this is not so much a test of solvency as a test of staying power under adversity. Times interest earned for 1995 for the Gillette Company was:

$$\text{Times Interest Earned} = \frac{\$1,296.9 \ + \ \$59.0}{\$59.0} = 23x$$

Market-Related and Dividend Ratios

Two ratios are affected by the market price for shares of ownership in corporations. These are the price earnings ratio and the dividend yield ratio. In addition, analysts sometimes calculate a dividend payout ratio as a measure of the degree to which the firm is likely to be able to continue its dividend payments provided there is fluctuation in future income.

Price Earnings Ratio (PE)

The relationship of the market price of shares of stock to the earnings of the company is of great interest to investors. Companies that are growing rapidly and are thought to have good potential for future growth often find that their shares are traded at a multiple of earnings per share much higher than companies thought to have less promise. The price earnings ratio is often included in stock market tables in investment information prepared by analysts. The formula for this ratio is:

$$\text{Price Earnings Ratio (PE)} = \frac{\text{Market Price per Share of Stock}}{\text{Earnings per Share}}$$

Since the market price of shares frequently fluctuates, this ratio is sometimes calculated using an average market price for a period of time.

During 1995, the market price per share of stock in the Gillette Company was as low as $35.38 and as high as $55.38. Calculating a price earnings ratio using each of these figures shows that during the year, Gillette's price earnings ratio fluctuated between 19.1 and 29.9.

$$\text{1995 Low Price Earnings Ratio} = \frac{\$35.38}{\$1.85} = 19.1$$

$$\text{1995 High Price Earnings Ratio} = \frac{\$55.38}{\$1.85} = 29.9$$

Dividend Yield Ratio

The dividend yield to common shareholders is dependent upon the market price originally paid for the share and is calculated by dividing dividends received by the market price originally paid for the shares. For a prospective investor, dividend yield is the dividend per share divided by the current market price of the stock.

$$\text{Dividend Yield} = \frac{\text{Dividends per Share}}{\text{Market Price per Share}}$$

If the market price of shares in the Gillette Company was $55, the dividend yield in 1995 when dividends per share of $.60 were paid to shareholders would have been:

$$\text{Dividend Yield} = \frac{\$.60}{\$55} = 1.1\%$$

Dividend Payout

The dividend payout ratio shows the proportion of net income that was paid in dividends. Both the dividend yield and dividend payout ratio are useful for forecasting future dividend streams to investors in the company's common stock. The formula for this ratio is:

$$\text{Dividend Payout} = \frac{\text{Dividends}}{\text{Net Income (available to common stockholders)}}$$

For the Gillette Company in 1995, dividends paid to common stockholders totaled $266.3 million, therefore the dividend payout was:

$$\text{Dividend Payout} = \frac{\$266.3}{\$818.8} = 33\%$$

Using Ratios to Think about Management Strategies

Sometimes it is useful when conducting a financial analysis to think about the interrelationships between ratios and to use them to think about the strategies that management has adopted or might adopt. One well-known algebraic construction using ratios is known as the *du Pont model* because financial analysts at the E. I. du Pont de Nemours & Co. are credited with its development and use during the 1920s. The du Pont model multiplies profit margin times asset turnover times a ratio of assets over equity to calculate return on shareholders' equity. If we look at this algebraic construction, we can see why it is so useful.

$$\frac{\text{Income}}{\text{Sales}} \text{ x } \frac{\text{Sales}}{\text{Assets}} \text{ x } \frac{\text{Assets}}{\text{Owners' Equity}} = \text{Return on Owners' Equity}$$

The first ratio, profit margin, can be used to focus management's attention on the relationship between the price and cost of products or services sold. The second ratio, asset turnover, emphasizes the efficient use of resources in producing products and services. The third ratio, assets over equity, focuses on the ability of management to leverage the firm properly to provide maximum return to shareholders. Each of these major classes of decisions that managers must make can be examined in light of its ability to provide the overall objective of increasing return to shareholders.

Common Size Financial Statements

In order to examine changing financial structure of a firm through time and the changing nature of operations, many analysts like to create common size financial statements in which the statement of financial position and the statement of income are prepared in the percentage format. In a common size balance sheet, each asset, liability, and owner's equity amount is expressed as a percentage of total assets. In a common size statement of income, sales is set at 100%, and each item is expressed as a percentage of sales.

Common size financial statements facilitate the comparison of firms of a different size as well. Although firms may be in the same industry, they may be of significantly different sizes, and common size statements allow an analyst to focus on the efficiency with which managements of different firms have created a capital structure and have achieved efficient operations.

Common size statements of financial position and statements of income for the Gillette Company are presented in **Exhibit 2**.

Exhibit 1   The Gillette Company and Subsidiary Companies—Consolidated Statement of Income and Earnings Reinvested in the Business for Years Ended December 31, 1995, 1994, and 1993 ($ million, except per share amounts)

	1995	1994	1993
Net sales	$6,794.7	$6,070.2	$5,410.8
Cost of sales	2,540.2	2,221.9	2,044.3
Gross profit	4,254.5	3,848.3	3,366.5
Selling, General and Administrative Expenses	2,883.2	2,621.6	2,279.2
Realignment expense	----	----	262.6
Profit from operations	1,371.3	1,226.7	824.7
Nonoperating charges (income)			
Interest income	(9.9)	(19.0)	(27.3)
Interest expense	59.0	61.1	59.8
Other charges-net	25.3	80.5	109.5
	74.4	122.6	142.0
Income before income taxes and cumulative effect of accounting changes	1,296.9	1,104.1	682.7
Income taxes	473.4	405.8	255.8
Income before cumulative effect of accounting changes	823.5	698.3	426.9
Cumulative effect of accounting changes	---	---	(138.6)
Net income	823.5	698.3	288.3
Preferred stock dividends, net of tax benefit	4.7	4.7	4.7
Net income available to common stockholders	818.8	693.6	283.6
Earnings reinvested in the business at beginning of year	2,830.2	2,357.9	2,259.6
	3,649.0	3,051.5	2,543.2
Common stock dividends declared	266.3	221.3	185.3
Earnings reinvested in the business at end of year	$3,382.7	$2,830.2	$2,357.9
Income per common share before cumulative effect of accounting changes	$ 1.85	$ 1.57	$.96
Cumulative effect of accounting changes	---	---	(.32)
Net income per common share	$1.85	$1.57	$.64
Dividends declared per common share	$.60	$.50	$.42
Weighted average number of common shares outstanding (millions)	443.5	442.3	440.9

Exhibit 1 (continued)   The Gillette Company and Subsidiary Companies—Consolidated Balance Sheets, December 31, 1995 and 1994 ($ millions)

	1995	1994
Assets		
Current assets		
Cash and cash equivalents	$ 47.9	$43.8
Short-term investments, at cost, which approximate market value	1.6	2.3
Receivables, less allowances: 1995-$59.2; 1994-$52.1	1,659.5	1,379.5
Inventories	1,035.1	941.2
Deferred income taxes	220.2	220.6
Prepaid expenses	140.2	113.0
Total current assets	3,104.5	2,700.4
Property, plant and equipment, at cost less accumulated depreciation	1,636.9	1,411.0
Intangible assets, less accumulated amortization	1,221.4	887.4
Other assets	377.5	314.6
	$6,340.3	$5,313.4
Liabilities and stockholders' equity		
Current liabilities		
Loans payable	$576.2	$344.4
Current portion of long-term debt	26.5	28.1
Accounts payable and accrued liabilities	1,273.3	1,178.2
Income taxes	248.0	185.5
Total current liabilities	2,124.0	1,736.2
Long-term debt	691.1	715.1
Deferred income taxes	72.7	53.1
Other long-term liabilities	919.2	774.3
Minority interest	20.0	17.4
Stockholders' equity		
8.0% Cumulative Series C ESOP Convertible Preferred, without par value, issued: 1995-160,701 shares; 1994 - 162,928 shares	96.9	98.2
Unearned ESOP compensation	(34.3)	(44.2)
Common stock, par value $1 per share		
Authorized 1,160,000,000 shares; Issued: 1995-559,718,438 shares; 1994-558,242,404 shares	559.7	558.2
Additional paid-in capital	31.1	(1.4)
Earnings reinvested in the business	3,382.7	2,830.2
Cumulative foreign currency translation adjustments	(477.0)	(377.1)
Treasury stock, at cost: 1995-115,254,353 shares; 1994-115,343,404 shares	(1,045.8)	(1,046.6
Total stockholders' equity	2,513.3	2,017.3
	$6,340.3	$5,313.4

Exhibit 1 (continued) The Gillette Company and Subsidiary Companies—Consolidated Statements of Cash Flows for Years Ended December 31, 1995, 1994, and 1993. ($ millions)

	1995	1994	1993
Operating activities			
Net income	$823.5	$698.3	$288.3
Adjustments to reconcile net income to net cash provided by operating activities:			
Cumulative effect of accounting changes	---	---	138.6
Provision for realignment expense	---	---	164.1
Depreciation and amortization	248.4	215.4	218.5
Other	(3.1)	15.1	51.8
Changes in assets and liabilities, net of effects from acquisition of businesses:			
Accounts receivable	(286.1)	(147.4)	(101.8)
Inventories	(94.1)	(66.7)	(56.0)
Accounts payable and accrued liabilities	67.0	93.7	10.8
Other working capital items	60.7	37.4	(30.7)
Other noncurrent assets and liabilities	4.2	(40.3)	48.1
Net cash provided by operating activities	820.5	805.5	731.7
Investing activities			
Additions to property, plant and equipment	(471.1)	(399.8)	(352.0)
Disposals of property, plant and equipment	30.0	24.9	10.2
Acquisition of businesses, less cash acquired	(276.7)	(25.6)	(452.9)
Other	12.1	16.9	(35.6)
Net cash used in investing activities	(705.7)	(383.6)	(830.3)
Financing activities			
Proceeds from exercise of stock option and purchase plans	31.6	18.4	24.5
Proceeds from long-term debt	---	---	500.0
Reduction of long-term debt	(19.6)	(200.7)	(414.8)
Increase (decrease) in loans payable	133.6	(12.9)	177.5
Dividends paid	(259.7)	(217.1)	(183.3)
Net cash provided by (used in) financing activities	(114.1)	(412.3)	103.9
Effect of exchange rate changes on cash	3.4	(2.9)	(3.5)
Increase in cash and cash equivalents	4.1	6.7	1.8
Cash and cash equivalents at beginning of year	43.8	37.1	35.3
Cash and cash equivalents at end of year	$ 47.9	$ 43.8	$ 37.1
Supplemental disclosure of cash paid for :			
Interest	$62.4	$61.6	$72.5
Income taxes	$289.1	$240.6	$180.9
Noncash investing and financing activities:			
Acquisition of businesses			
Fair value of assets acquired	$394.9	$19.0	$705.8
Cash paid	278.3	25.6	481.1
Liabilities assumed	$116.6	$(6.6)	$224.7

Exhibit 2   The Gillette Company and Subsidiary Companies—Common Size Statement of Income
for the Years Ended December 31, 1994, 1994 and 1993 (%)

	1995	1994	1993
Net sales	100.0%	100.0%	100.0%
Cost of sales	37.4	36.6	37.8
Gross Profit	62.6%	63.4%	62.2%
Selling, general and administrative expenses	42.4	43.2	42.1
Realignment expense	---	- --	4.9
Profit from Operations	20.2%	20.2%	15.2%
Nonoperating charges (income)			
Interest income	(.1)	(.3)	(.5)
Interest expense	.8	1.0	1.1
Other charges - net	.4	1.3	2.0
	1.1%	2.0%	2.6%
Income before income taxes and cumulative effect of accounting changes	19.1	18.2	12.6
Income taxes	7.0	6.7	4.7
Income before cumulative effect of accounting changes	12.1%	11.5%	7.9%
Cumulative effect of accounting changes	---	---	(2.6)
Net income	12.1%	11.5%	5.3%

Exhibit 2 (continued)   The Gillette Company and Subsidiary Companies—Common Size Balance
Sheets December 31, 1994 and 1994 (%)

	1995	1994
Assets		
Current Assets		
Cash and cash equivalents	.8%	.8%
Short-term investments, at cost, which approximates market value	--	--
Receivables, less allowances	26.2	26.0
Inventories	16.3	17.7
Deferred income taxes	3.5	4.2
Prepaid expenses	2.2	2.1
Total current assets	49.0%	50.8%
Property, plant and equipment, at cost less accumulated depreciation	25.8	26.6
Intangible assets, less accumulated amortization	19.3	16.7
Other assets	5.9	5.9
	100.0%	100.0%
Liabilities and stockholders' equity		
Current liabilities		
Loans payable	9.1%	6.5%
Current portion of long-term debt	.4	.5
Accounts payable and accrued liabilities	20.1	22.2
Income taxes	3.9	3.5
Total current liabilities	33.5%	32.7%
Long-term debt	10.9	13.5
Deferred income taxes	1.1	1.0
Other long-term liabilities	14.5	14.6
Minority interest	.3	.3
Stockholders' equity		
8.0% Cumulative Series C ESOP Convertible Preferred, without par value, Issued: 1995-160,701 shares; 1994-162,928 shares	1.5	1.8
Unearned ESOP compensation	(.5)	(.8)
Common stock, par value $1 per share		
Authorized 1,160,000,000 shares		
Issued: 1995-559,718,438 shares; 1994-558,242,410 shares	8.8	10.5
Additional paid-in capital	.5	--
Earnings reinvested in the business	53.4	53.3
Cumulative foreign currency translation adjustments	(7.5)	(7.1)
Treasury stock, at cost: 1994-115,254,353 shares; 1994-115,343,404 shares	(16.5)	(19.7)
Total stockholders' equity	39.6%	38.0%
	100.0%	100.0%